A GUIDE TO

THE OWL SERVICE

MARY HARTLEY

WITH TONY BUZAN

Hodder & Stoughton

Mind Maps: Anne Jones
Illustrations: Karen Donnelly

ISBN 0 340 67959 X

First published 1998
Impression number   10 9 8 7 6 5 4 3 2 1
Year   2002 2001 2000 1999 1998

The 'Teach Yourself' name and logo are registered trade marks of
Hodder & Stoughton Ltd.

Typeset by Transet Limited, Coventry, England.
Printed in Great Britain for Hodder & Stoughton Educational, a division of
Hodder Headline Plc, 338 Euston Road, London NW1 3BH by Cox and Wyman Ltd,
Reading, Berks.

CONTENTS

There are five important things you must know about your brain and memory to revolutionise
the way you study:

◆ how your memory
   ('recall') works *while* you are learning
◆ how your memory works *after* you have finished learning
◆ how to use Mind Maps – a special technique for helping you
   with all aspects of your studies
◆ how to increase your reading speed
◆ how to prepare for tests and exams.

Recall during learning
– THE NEED FOR BREAKS

When you are studying, your memory
can concentrate, understand and
remember well for between 20 and 45
minutes at a time. Then it needs a break.
If you carry on for longer than this
without a break your memory starts to
break down. If you study for hours non-stop, you will remember
only a small fraction of what you have been trying to learn, and
you will have wasted hours of valuable time.

So, ideally, *study for less than an hour*, then take a five to ten
minute break. During the break listen to music, go for a walk, do
some exercise, or just daydream. (Daydreaming is a necessary
brain-power booster – geniuses do it regularly.) During the break
your brain will be sorting out what it has been learning, and you
will go back to your books with the new information safely
stored and organised in your memory banks. We recommend
breaks at regular intervals as you work through the Literature
Guides. Make sure you take them!

Recall after learning
— THE WAVES OF YOUR MEMORY

What do you think begins to happen to your
memory straight after you have finished learning something?
Does it immediately start forgetting? No! Your brain actually
increases its power and carries on remembering. For a short
time after your study session, your brain integrates the
information, making a more complete picture of everything it
has just learnt. Only then does the rapid decline in memory
begin, and as much as 80 per cent of what you have learnt can
be forgotten in a day.

However, if you catch the top of the wave of your memory, and
briefly review (look back over) what you have been studying at
the correct time, the memory is stamped in far more strongly,
and stays at the crest of the wave for a much longer time. To
maximise your brain's power to remember, take a few minutes
and use a Mind Map to review what you have learnt at the end
of a day. Then review it at the end of a week, again at the end
of a month, and finally a week before your test or exam. That
way you'll ride your memory
wave all the way there – and beyond!

The Mind Map ®
— A PICTURE OF THE WAY YOU THINK

Do you like taking notes? More importantly, do you like having to
go back over and learn them before tests or exams? Most
students I know certainly do not! And how do you take your
notes? Most people take notes on lined paper, using blue or
black ink. The result, visually, is boring! And what does *your* brain
do when it is bored? It turns off, tunes out, and goes to sleep!
Add a dash of colour, rhythm, imagination, and the whole note-
taking process becomes much more fun, uses more of your
brain's abilities, and improves your recall and understanding.

A Mind Map mirrors the way your brain works. It can be used
for note-taking from books or in class, for reviewing what you
have just studied, and for essay planning for coursework and in
tests or exams. It uses all your memory's natural techniques to
build up your rapidly growing 'memory muscle'.

You will find Mind Maps throughout this book. Study them, add some colour, personalise them, and then have a go at drawing your own – you'll remember them far better! Stick them in your files and on your walls for a quick-and-easy review of the topic.

HOW TO DRAW A MIND MAP

1 Start in the middle of the page. This gives your brain the maximum room for its thoughts.
2 Always start by drawing a small picture or symbol. Why? Because a picture is worth a thousand words to your brain. And try to use at least three colours, as colour helps your memory even more.
3 Let your thoughts flow, and write or draw your ideas on coloured branching lines connected to your central image. These key symbols and words are the headings for your topic. Start like the Mind Map on page 9.
4 Then add facts and ideas by drawing more, smaller, branches on to the appropriate main branches, just like a tree.
5 Always print your word clearly on its line. Use only one word per line.
6 To link ideas and thoughts on different branches, use arrows, colours, underlining, and boxes (see page 13).

HOW TO READ A MIND MAP

1 Begin in the centre, the focus of your topic.
2 The words/images attached to the centre are like chapter headings, read them next.
3 Always read out from the centre, in every direction (even on the left-hand side, where you will have to read from right to left, instead of the usual left to right).

USING MIND MAPS

Mind Maps are a versatile tool – use them for taking notes in class or from books, for solving problems, for brainstorming with friends, and for reviewing and working for tests or exams – their uses are endless! You will find them invaluable for planning essays for coursework and exams. Number your main branches in the order in which you want to use them and off you go – the main headings for your essay are done and all your ideas are logically organised!

Super speed reading

It seems incredible, but it's been proved – the faster you read, the more you understand and remember! So here are some tips to help you to practise reading faster – you'll cover the ground more quickly, remember more, and have more time left for both work and play.

◆ First read the whole text (whether it's a lengthy book or an exam or test paper) very quickly, to give your brain an overall idea of what's ahead and get it working. (It's like sending out a scout to look at the territory you have to cover – it's much easier when you know what to expect!) Then read the text again for more detailed information.
◆ Have the text a reasonable distance away from your eyes. In this way your eye/brain system will be able to see more at a glance, and will naturally begin to read faster.
◆ Take in groups of words at a time. Rather than reading 'slowly and carefully' read faster, more enthusiastically.
◆ Take in phrases rather than single words while you read.
◆ Use a guide. Your eyes are designed to follow movement, so a thin pencil underneath the lines you are reading, moved smoothly along, will 'pull' your eyes to faster speeds.

Preparing for tests and exams

◆ Review your work systematically. Cram at the start of your course, not the end, and avoid 'exam panic'!
◆ Use Mind Maps throughout your course, and build a Master Mind Map for each subject – a giant Mind Map that summarises everything you know about the subject.
◆ Use memory techniques such as mnemonics (verses or systems for remembering things like dates and events).
◆ Get together with one or two friends to study, compare Mind Maps, and discuss topics.

AND FINALLY...

Have *fun* while you learn – it has been shown that students who make their studies enjoyable understand and remember everything better and get the highest grades. I wish you and your brain every success!

(Tony Buzan)

HOW TO USE THIS GUIDE

This guide assumes that you have read *The Owl Service*, although you could read 'Background' and 'The story of *The Owl Service*' before that. It is best to use the guide alongside the novel. You could read the 'Who's who?' and 'Themes' sections without referring to the novel, but you will get more out of these sections if you do refer to it to check the points made, especially when thinking about the questions designed to test your recall and help you think about the novel.

The different sections

The 'Commentary' section can be used in a number of ways. One way is to read a chapter or part of a chapter in the novel, and then read the commentary for that section. Keep on until you come to test yourself exercise – then have a break! Alternatively, read the commentary for a chapter or part of a chapter, then read the section in the novel, then go back to the commentary. Find out what works best for you.

'Topics for discussion and brainstorming' gives topics that could well feature in exams or provide the basis for coursework. It would be particularly useful for you to discuss them with friends, or brainstorm them using Mind Map techniques (see p. iv).

'How to get an "A" in English Literature' gives valuable advice on what to look for in any text, and what skills you need to develop in order to achieve your personal best.

'The exam essay' is a useful 'night before' reminder of how to tackle exam questions, and 'Model answer' gives an example of an A-grade essay and the Mind Map and plan used to write it.

The questions

Whenever you come across a question in the guide, with a star ✪ in front of it, think about it for a moment. You could even jot down a few words in rough to focus your mind. There is not usually a 'right' answer to these questions: it is important for you to develop your own opinions if you want to get an 'A'. The 'Test yourself' sections are designed to take you about 10-20 minutes each – which will be time well spent. Take a short break after each one.

Page numbers

Page references are to the Lions Paperback edition. If you have another edition, the page numbers may be slightly different, although the chapters will be the same.

KEY TO ICONS

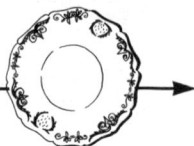

Themes and imagery

A **theme** is an idea explored by an author. **Imagery** refers to the kind of word picture used to make the idea come alive. Particular sorts of image are usually associated with each theme. Whenever a theme is dealt with in the guide, the appropriate icon is used. This means you can find where a theme is just by flicking through the book. Go on – try it now!

Love
  and betrayal

Cultural identity

Class

Myth, magic
  and reality

Parents
  and children

STYLE AND LANGUAGE

This heading and icon are used in the Commentary wherever there is a special section on the author's choice of words and use of literary devices.

BACKGROUND

About the author

Alan Garner was born in Congleton, Cheshire in 1934. He grew up in the Cheshire village Alderley Edge, in a working-class family. Events in the first part of his life had the effect of separating him from his traditional family roots. At primary school, the teachers forced him to drop the Cheshire dialect his family spoke, and when he won a place at Manchester Grammar School he found himself rejecting his family's values and way of life. However, after doing his National Service in the Royal Artillery and going to Magdalen College, Oxford to study Classics, he returned to Cheshire to live near Alderley Edge and began his first book.

About his books

These experiences emerge in Alan Garner's work, and you will see them in *The Owl Service*, for example in the questions it raises about identity, and its roots in ancient myth and tragedy. Another important experience was a series of childhood illnesses which kept him in bed for about ten years. Alan Garner thinks he may have started writing to create the life that he couldn't live as a child. He loved reading *The Beano* and *Dandy*, and chose to write for children because children are still discovering the universe and have a freshness of vision not shared by all adults.

Although Alan Garner's books are written for children, his development as a writer shows them increasing in power and complexity. Their blend of fantasy and realism, as myth breaks through into the modern world, and their awareness of the timelessness of emotional experience create an emotional impact which makes his books demanding and rewarding.

The Owl Service

The Owl Service was published in 1967 and won the Carnegie Medal and the Guardian Award for Children's Fiction. Alan

Garner got the idea for the book when a friend showed him a dinner service with a pattern which could be arranged to make pictures of owls or flowers. He immediately thought of an old story he knew, one of a medieval collection of Welsh myths known as The *Mabinogion*.

Myth and legend

A **myth** is an ancient traditional story not generally held to be literally true. A **legend** is a story which is thought to be based on historical fact, to some extent at least. ✪ Is the story of Lleu, Blodeuwedd and Gronw myth or legend? Think about this as you read the novel.

The Old Story of the Mabinogion

The story concerns a magician, Gwydion, and his half-sister Arianrod. Against her wishes she gives birth magically to a son, Lleu, who is cared for by Gwydion. Lleu has the status of a god, and is associated with the sun. With the help of the enchanter Math, Gwydion makes a wife for Lleu out of the flowers of the meadowsweet, the oak and the broom. They do this because Arianrod has placed curses on Lleu, one of which said that he could never have a mortal wife. The flower wife is called Blodeuwedd. She falls in love with Gronw Pebyr, and the two of them conspire to get rid of Lleu.

It is part of Lleu's destiny that he can die only under certain conditions. Blodeuwedd finds out from him what these conditions are and tells Gronw. Gronw uses this knowledge and kills Lleu with a spear, as he thinks, but Lleu doesn't die. As the spear goes through him he screams and turns into an eagle. One day a sow indicates to Gwydion that Lleu is in an oak tree, and Gwydion charms Lleu down with song and makes him human again. Lleu then kills Gronw. Gwydion punishes Blodeuwedd by turning her into an owl, hated by other birds and condemned to hunt at night.

HOW IT APPEARS IN THE OWL SERVICE

In *The Owl Service* the story of Lleu, Blodeuwedd and Gronw is acted out whenever the power unleashed by the act of making a living woman out of flowers builds up and is expressed through the making of flowers, as Blodeuwedd was made, or owls, like the bird she was turned into. Gwyn, Alison and Roger are the three people in the present generation who are forced to suffer the emotional turmoil of the ancient myth. The tensions and jealousies in their relationship recall the bitter triangle of Lleu, Blodeuwedd and Gronw. This is enhanced by their names: Gwyn was one of the names of Lleu, Alison is a flower name (Blodeuwedd was made of flowers), and Roger means famous with the spear (Gronw kills Lleu with a spear).

Understanding the relationship between the modern story and the legend will increase your appreciation of the novel. However, don't read *The Owl Service* just as an updated legend. It stands in its own right as a powerful and well-crafted account of complex emotional relationships.

THE STORY OF THE OWL SERVICE

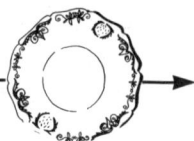

Ancient passions

The Owl Service tells **three stories** which unfold at the same time. The oldest narrative is the tale of **Blodeuwedd**, **Lleu** and **Gronw**, which you will find detailed in the first section of this book. It is an ancient tale of love and jealousy, of two men who loved the same woman and finally killed each other, leaving her to endure a bitter **punishment** for her **betrayal** of her husband. The power of their suffering is contained within the secluded valley, and from time to time builds up until it is released through another group of two men and a woman who are destined to undergo the same experience as the original three. The signal that the story is to be played out again is the **appearance** of Blodeuwedd as either **owls** or **flowers**.

The older generation

The second narrative shows how this happened to **Nancy**, **Huw** and **Bertram**. Bertram was the **master** of the big house in the valley in which the story is set. Nancy was a **servant** in the house and she and Bertram fell in love and planned to marry, in spite of the class difference between them. Their relationship enraged **Huw**, who also loved Nancy. To pay Bertram back for this and for making a fool of him by riding his **motorbike** at him, causing him to jump, he removed the brake blocks from the motorbike, hoping to see him land in the rhododendrons. Bertram, however, rode it up the mountain pass and was killed.

In an attempt to stop the source of the power Huw and Nancy covered up the painting of Blodeuwedd in the billiard room with pebble dash and hid the plates in the **loft**. These plates were decorated with a pattern which may be owls or flowers, and were painted by Huw's **grandfather** in an earlier attempt to harness the dangerous power. Another attempt to stop it was made by **Bertram** when he shot the owl which is now locked in a stable room. Huw carried on living in the valley and working in the house. Nancy and the son she had by Huw, **Gwyn**, went to live in **Aberystwyth**. She returns to the house when she is asked to be cook for the summer for Bertram's relatives, who now own the house, and brings Gwyn with her.

The young generation

The third narrative focuses on **Alison**, **Gwyn** and **Roger**, three adolescents who are thrown together for the summer. Alison is the **daughter** of Margaret, who married Bertram's **cousin**. The house has passed from Bertram to his cousin, and when he died, to Alison, its new owner. Margaret is now married to **Clive**, father of Roger. The newly formed family is having its first holiday together in the house.

The personal relationship between Alison, Gwyn and Roger is characterised by **tensions** and **jealousy**. Gwyn is from a different social background from Roger and Alison but is cleverer than they are. He and Alison are close, and this upsets the relationship between her and Roger. The tension increases as Alison becomes the source through which the ancient power is once again released. When they find the hidden **plates** and Alison feels compelled to make the pattern into owls, **Nancy** is filled with consternation and fears another tragedy. She finally leaves the house, trying to take **Gwyn** with her.

Gwyn himself tries to leave when he thinks Alison has betrayed him to Roger, by laughing with him at Gwyn's confidences about his attempts to 'improve' himself. Gwyn, however, is destined to stay. He is guided by Huw in piecing together the elements of the ancient myth which they are now experiencing, discovering in the process that **Huw** is his **father**. The power builds up as the association of **Alison** and **Blodeuwedd** becomes stronger and she suffers as Blodeuwedd suffered until Roger releases her from its grip by recognising that she should have made the pattern on the plates into **flowers** instead of **owls**. Peace is restored to the valley.

HOW WELL HAVE YOU REMEMBERED THE PLOT?

Try to fill in the missing words from this summary without looking back at the original. Feel free to use your own words if they have the same meaning.

Ancient passions

The Owl Service tells _____ _____which unfold at the
same time. The oldest narrative is the tale of _____, _____
and _____. It is an ancient tale of love and jealousy, of two
men who loved the same woman and finally killed each other,
leaving her to endure a bitter _____ for her_____ of her
husband. The power of their suffering is contained within the
secluded valley, and from time to time builds up until it is
released through another group of two men and a woman who
are destined to undergo the same experience as the original
three. The signal that the story is to be played out again is the
appearance of Blodeuwedd as either_____ or _____.

The older generation

The second narrative shows how this happened to _____,
_____ and _____. Bertram was the _____ of the big
house in the valley in which the story is set. Nancy was a
_____ in the house and she and Bertram fell in love and
planned to marry, in spite of the class difference between
them. Their relationship enraged _____, who also loved
Nancy. To pay Bertram back for this and for making a fool of
him by riding his_____at him, causing him to jump, he
removed the brake blocks from the motorbike, hoping to see
him land in the rhodedendrons. Bertram, however, rode it up
the mountain pass and was killed.

In an attempt to stop the source of the power Huw and Nancy
covered up the painting of Blodeuwedd in the billiard room
with pebble-dash and hid the plates in the _____. These
plates were decorated with a pattern which may be owls or
flowers, and were painted by Huw's _____ in an earlier
attempt to harness the dangerous power. Another attempt to
stop it was made by _____ when he shot the owl which is
now locked in a stable room. Huw carried on living in the
valley and working in the house. Nancy and the son she had
by Huw, _____, went to live in_____. She returns to the
house when she is asked to be cook for the summer for
Bertram's relatives who now own the house, and brings Gwyn
with her.

The young generation

The third narrative focuses on _____, _____ and _____,
three adolescents who are thrown together for the summer.
Alison is the _____ of Margaret, who married Bertram's
_____ The house has passed from Bertram to his cousin, and
when he died, to Alison, its new owner. Margaret is now
married to_____, father of Roger. The newly formed family is
having its first holiday together in the house.

The personal relationship between Alison, Gwyn and Roger is
characterised by _____ and _____. Gwyn is from a
different social background from Roger and Alison but is
cleverer than they are. He and Alison are close,and this upsets
the realtionship between her and Roger. The tension increases
as Alison becomes the source through which the ancient
power is once again released. When they find the hidden
_____ and Alison feels compelled to make the pattern into
owls, _____ is filled with consternation and fears another
tragedy. She finally leaves the house, trying to take _____
with her.

Gwyn himself tries to leave when he thinks Alison has
betrayed him to Roger, by laughing with him at Gwyn's
confidences about his attempts to 'improve' himself. Gwyn,
however, is destined to stay. He is guided by Huw in piecing
together the elements of the ancient myth which they are now
experiencing, discovering in the process that _____ is his
_____. The power builds up as the association of _____
and _____ becomes stronger and she suffers as Blodeuwedd
suffered until Roger releases her from its grip by recognising
that she should have made the plates into _____ instead of
_____. Peace is restored to the valley.

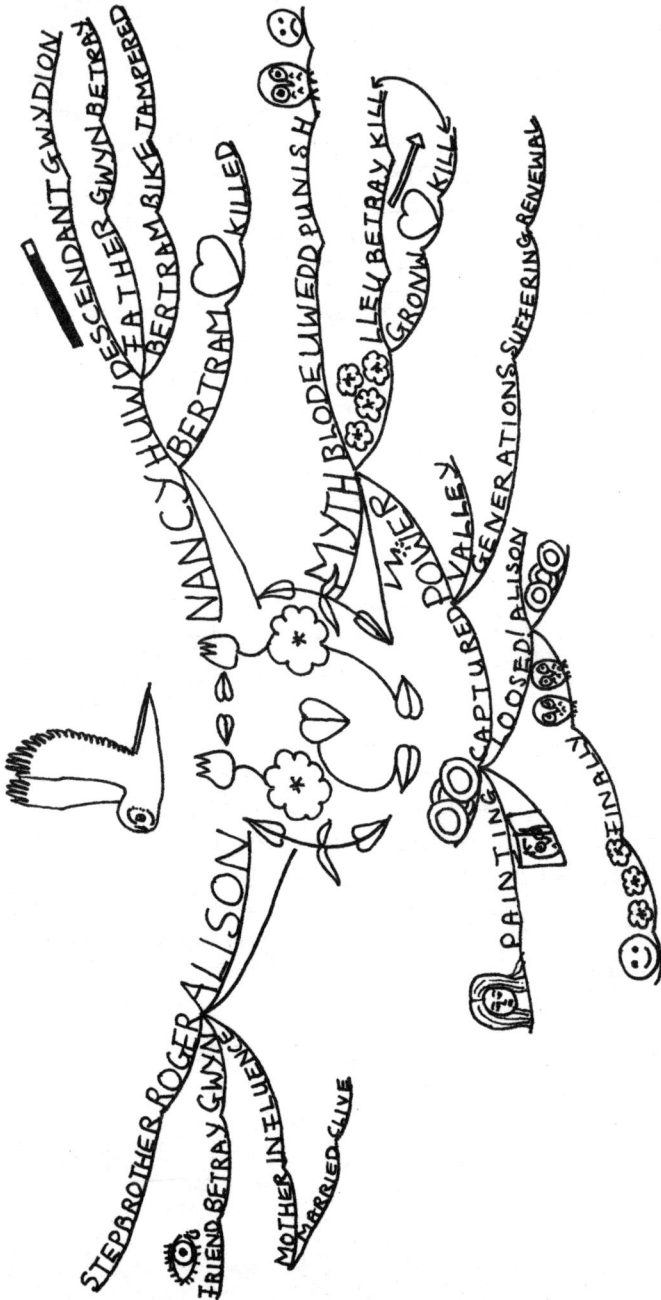

The story of *The Owl Service* shown on a Mind Map

WHO'S WHO

As you read these outlines, try to create the characters in your own imagination. Picture how they would look, dress, speak and behave. This will add to your enjoyment and help your memory.

Alison

Alison is torn between her friendship with Gwyn and her mother's wishes. She is careful not to upset her mother, and she is very shaken when Margaret is angry with her: *'I didn't know she could be like that'* (p. 76). She accepts that she will do what Margaret wants, for example, when she leaves school. Alison enjoys activities like the choir and the tennis club, and is very aware of her social status and her new position as owner of the house. In spite of owning the house she doesn't feel she belongs in the valley, and envies Gwyn: *'You came a week ago, and you know everything as if you'd always lived here'* (p. 74).

Alison feels affection and compassion for Gwyn when she realises how he has to struggle for the opportunities she takes for granted. Her telling Roger about this is naive and thoughtless. Alison's thoughtlessness may be seen as cruel when she speaks slightingly of Clive to Roger – *'Clive's sweet, but he's a bit of a rough diamond, isn't he?'* (p. 111) – and her attitude to Nancy is arrogant. Although she is weak , Alison

9

can manipulate relationships to her advantage, as in the way she keeps on Clive's good side by constantly calling him sweet and hiding the fact that she considers him to be of a lower social status than herself and her mother.

Gwyn

Gwyn is a fiery and volatile character, with a quick and active intelligence and a facility with words and language. Much of Gwyn's humour comes from his ability to coin phrases. He is the illegitimate son of Nancy and Huw, the first person in his family to be formally educated. He is very aware of the differences between his background and Alison's and Roger's. Sometimes he uses it to hurt, as when he mockingly says *Miss Alison* and that he'll use the tradesman's entrance (p. 77), but this disguises Gwyn's own hurt and his vulnerability. Gwyn is also confused about his Welsh background. He is part of the Welsh tradition and culture, but aware of its domination by the English and anxious not to be considered a *Taff* (p. 102).

Gwyn is loyal to Nancy and scared of what she can do. He makes light of her rough treatment of him: *'And what's a clip on the earhole among friends?'* (p. 26). He feels close to Alison – *'With you it all goes how I mean it'* (p. 76) – which makes his anguish when he thinks she has betrayed him all the stronger.

Gwyn's sense of humour, his pride, his cleverness and his warmth win our sympathies throughout the book, so that we are shocked when at the end he remains cold and unforgiving. His dramatic change shows how much he has been hurt, and also is in keeping with what happens at the end of the legend.

Roger

Roger is a prosaic and unimaginative character. He looks for logical explanations of the strange events in the valley and uses dismissive terms like *hogwash* and *moonshine* (p. 112). His relationship with Gwyn is complex. He feels that the social, financial and emotional differences in their backgrounds make him superior to Gwyn, but at the same time he is a bit in awe of him and wants to be like him. Roger responds viciously when his offer of help is rejected by Gwyn: *'You make me puke'* (p. 38). He manages his confused feelings by dismissing Gwyn as a *'yob'* and uses the class system to unite Alison and himself against Gwyn: *'... He's not one of us'* (p. 112).

It is important for Roger to maintain a close relationship with Clive now that his mother has gone. We see his vulnerability where his mother is concerned in his reluctance to talk about her and his threat to hit Gwyn if he asks any more: *'If you open your big mouth once more I'll fill you in'* (p. 50). In the end it is Roger who shows the sensitivity and courage necessary to restore peace.

Huw

Huw is a mysterious figure. At times he seems simple and half-witted, but at other times what he says makes sense. Gwyn says *'There's too much that's screwy with him – and too much of it is sense'* (p. 75). Huw is steeped in the legends and history of his ancestors, and his conversation is full of references which confuse fact, legend, the present and the past. The cadences of his speech indicate that his first language is Welsh, and his poetic rhythms enhance the mysteriousness of his words. To the people of the valley he is respected as a prophet, and he plays a crucial part in guiding the events of the story to their conclusion.

Nancy

Nancy is a harsh and bitter character, driven by the events of the past. She is full of resentment that Bertram's death cheated her of her promised place as mistress of the big house, and cannot stand the way Alison in particular exercises authority over her. She hides from Gwyn who his father is, and becomes very agitated when Gwyn talks to Huw. She says she doesn't want him speaking Welsh and that she hasn't struggled to have him *talk like a labourer* (p. 16). At the same time she seems resentful of the education she enabled him to have. Nancy's ambitions for Gwyn are limited and she doesn't want his education to make a wider gap between them. She is full of anger for Huw, the *mad fool* who caused Bertram's death.

Clive

Clive comes from a different social class from Margaret, his new wife. He has made money through business, rather than inheriting it. His habit of speaking in clichés and generalities makes it difficult to see what he really thinks, although we know it is important to him that the new family gets on together. He is anxious that this holiday should be a success: *'And it is the first time we've all been together – as a family'* (p. 24). Clive wants a quiet life but also has to keep Margaret happy, which means he has to mediate between her and Nancy and Huw and has constantly to prevent Alison and Roger from upsetting her. Clive is kind to Alison, and obliging to Roger, buying him what he needs for his photography. Nevertheless, he can be harsh if Roger doesn't do as he wishes: *'We shan't expect any snotty-nosed kids who haven't learned their manners'* (p. 125).

Margaret

Margaret is a powerful presence in the book although we never meet her. She is snobbish, believing that social background is very important. She is used to getting her own way, and we see how she puts pressure on others to make sure her wishes prevail: *'She's a bit upset'* (p. 21); *'Your mother's very upset'* (p. 23); *'Remember what Margaret said, won't you?'* (p. 73); *'Mummy was upset yesterday, and Mummy was upset the day before, and I bet you anything Mummy will be upset today'*. (p. 91). Perhaps her desire to keep Alison away from Gwyn is a guilty secret about Alison's parentage, but it is as likely to be because she thinks Gwyn's background makes him an unsuitable friend. Clive is not of the same class as Margaret, and Roger suggests she married him for his money.

Test yourself

Make your own Mind Map, family tree or web of the characters and their interrelationships. You can use the one on page 13 as a guide, if you like, but add your own images and colours.

The characters in the story

13

Love and betrayal

Love is a powerful force in each of the narratives. It caused Blodeuwedd to betray Lleu, and led to the deaths of Lleu and Gronw. Huw's love for Nancy and hers for Bertram led to Bertram's death. Nancy and Bertram fell in love and planned to marry in spite of the differences in their backgrounds and social situations. Nancy says that Bertram was a true gentleman (unlike Clive), and that he was ready to defy his family by marrying his servant. Nancy seems proud of his defiant attitude, and proud of herself for having captivated him: *just when I had him landed, high and dry* (p. 87).

Their relationship caused Huw intense misery and suffering. Huw wanted to make Bertram suffer by making a fool of him, removing the brake blocks from his motorbike to make him crash into the rhododendrons. Huw has to live with the guilty knowledge that his rival was killed as a result of this action, and has to endure the hatred of Nancy, the woman he loves and the mother of his son.

Nancy's anger and bitterness are directed at Huw, whose jealousy robbed her of the man she loved and her place as mistress of the house. The sound of the motorbike and the smell of petrol pervade the novel as reminders of the passion and betrayal experienced by Huw, Bertram and Nancy. The motorbike in the locked room and the buried brake blocks are tangible evidence of what happened.

Emotions in the three adolescents are less formed but still passionate and intense. Roger and Gwyn feel a mixture of liking and hatred for each other, and they are locked in rivalry over Alison. Roger resents Alison's closeness to Gwyn, and tries to draw her away from him by presenting Gwyn as an outsider, referring to Gwyn's working-class background and the way he speaks. We see the strong intimacy between Alison and Gwyn throughout the book, particularly in the afternoon they spend on the mountain (Chapters 16 and 17) and in the converation they have about the owls and the events in the valley. Gwyn trusts Alison and confides in her about his plans for the future. When Alison tells Roger what Gwyn has told her, Gwyn feels deeply hurt and betrayed. As he sees it, Alison has revealed his deepest feelings to his rival, and she and Roger have united in laughter against him. This act of betrayal wounds him as deeply as the spear wounded Lleu.

Clive and Margaret's marriage gives an example of a different kind of love. Margaret seems to be the dominant force in the marriage, imposing her will through a series of strategies such as having headaches and being upset. The desertion of Clive and Roger by the *Birmingham Belle* is seen as the subject of gossip and scandal. It is fodder for the tabloid press, but at the same time it has hurt Roger deeply.

Class

Differences in social class are presented in a subtle way. We see aspects of the English class system in the inhabitants of the house. Margaret and Alison consider that they are of a higher social status than Clive and Roger. Clive seems to have been a travelling salesman at the start of his career, and it is suggested that he has 'bettered' himself by marrying Margaret. Alison's class superiority is effortless and ingrained. It is part of the reason she patronises Clive, and she uses it with casual viciousness when she attacks Roger. In spite of this division, Roger feels class solidarity with Alison, and uses it to strengthen their relationship and draw Alison away from Gwyn.

The 'masters' in the book are English; the 'servants' are Welsh. The Welsh are seen as an under-class, and the term 'Welsh' is used as a form of abuse. The English owners are secure in their position and assume superiority over those who work in the house and estate. Nancy's attitude to her class identity is ambivalent. She resents the fact that the family treats her in a superior way, but this is partly through her bitterness at having been robbed of her chance to improve her position. She doesn't want to change the system, but feels the unfairness of her situation: *I should be sitting at that table today saying potatoes was cold, not them* (p. 87). Nancy hates having to *bow and scrape* (p. 58) but would not mind the positions being reversed.

Nancy despises Clive because he wasn't born into the class she has become part of, and she relishes the way she tests him by giving him a knife and fork for his pear. She shows grudging admiration of Alison's position and the way she covered up for Clive. Nancy wants Gwyn to better himself, but only to a certain extent. Her ambitions and aspirations for Gwyn are limited to wanting him to do a non-manual job: *The other lads in our street wear overalls* (p. 92). She is proud of the fact that he is educated, but at the same time she resents it. She doesn't ant Gwyn to look down on her (p. 58).

Gwyn is ambitious for himself. He is educated and cultured, and recognises his own abilities. At the same time he acknowledges that he is Welsh and working-class, factors which he feels will prevent him from getting on in life. He is also hindered by Nancy's fear of him growing too far away from her. Gwyn's education has separated him from his class roots, and he suffers as a result.

Parents and children

The relationships between parents and children are complex and often painful. Clive, Margaret and Nancy all impose a different kind of pressure on their children, and the children react in different ways. Clive's desire to keep Margaret happy causes tension between him and Roger, which is usually kept at bay as the father and son cultivate a close relationship to compensate for Roger's mother's desertion. Roger has been hurt by his mother as Gwyn is hurt by his. In the legend on which the story is based, Lleu is cursed by his mother, Arianrod. Gwyn's feelings for Nancy are a mixture of anger, resentment and loyalty. The children inherit the burden of their parents' failure to deal with their problems.

Huw's role as a father is mysterious. As both Gwyn's natural father and his father in the legend, it is Huw's task to guide his son and to help him fulfil and survive his destiny. Gwyn doesn't understand why Nancy is so against Huw and wants to keep Gwyn away from him. Gwyn finds Huw a compelling figure, at times foolish and muddled, yet possessing a power and a position in the valley which is rooted in its past history. When Gwyn asks Nancy about Huw he is frustrated by her threats. Huw's eventual revelation to Gwyn that he is his father gives Gwyn the strength to defy Nancy and stay in the valley to embrace his fate.

Cultural identity

Gwyn's feelings about being Welsh are central to the novel. His wish to change the way he speaks and Nancy's dislike of him speaking Welsh focus on the way English dominates the Welsh culture. This is also seen in the attitude to the Welsh people shown by Clive, Roger and the earlier English owners of the house. However, the concept of 'Welshness' is far stronger than the concept of 'Englishness'. Although Gwyn dismisses Alison's prediction that he'll be a Professor of Welsh and says he will have to leave Wales (p. 92), he has a deep-rooted sense of belonging in the valley. He says that going to the valley was *like coming home* (p. 57). Alison points out that she has been spending holidays at the house all her life, but knows less about the valley than Gwyn does, even though he's only been there a week (p. 74). In spite of owning the house and the land, Alison and her family are strangers. They have no identity with the country they inhabit and exploit, unlike Gwyn and his ancestors.

Myth, magic and reality

The *Mabinogion* story is an essential part of the novel, influencing it at every point. The reader is drawn into the story and its meaning for the present generation as the pieces are gradually pieced together and the strange events in the valley begin to form a meaningful pattern.

The novel combines realism with the forces of magic and the supernatural. Although the three young people are destined to fulfil their roles as the representatives of the ancient legend, they are at the same time believable contemporary figures. The relationship between them is expressed powerfully and realistically. We sense the emotional tensions between them as they suffer recognisable adolescent emotions such as hurt, embarrassment, anger, humiliation and jealousy. Their feelings are raw and strong, made more intense by the claustrophobic feeling evoked as they spend the summer cooped up together. Their passions and their vulnerability make them likely candidates for the valley's power. They provide the energy which activates the working of the old story, in the same kind of way as poltergeists are said to be activated by adolescent sexual energy. The same may be said of figures such as the woman Gwyn sees in the marh, and the reflection of Blodeuwedd in the fish tank. You might think of these apparitions as coming from an external source, or as being created by the human mind.

Often the realistic and the magical merge together, as when Gwyn and Alison are trapped by the methane gas (Chapter 11). As Gwyn points out, there is a logical reason for the flames' appearance. However, as Alison says, there may be a supernatural force harnessing and using the natural phenomenon.

once you've absorbed the different themes, take a break before going on to the Commentary

The development of the main themes

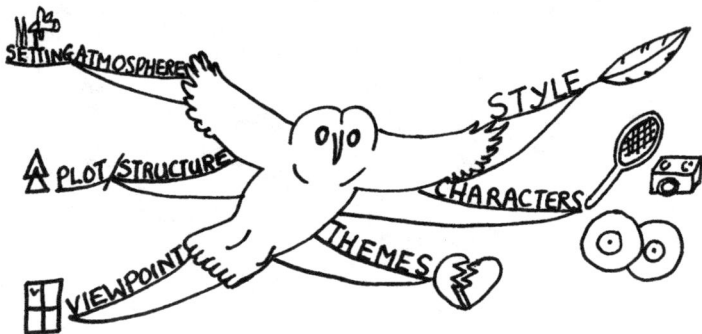

The Commentary divides the chapters into short sections, beginning with a brief preview which will prepare you for the section and help in last-minute revision. The Commentary comments on whatever is important in the section, focusing on the areas shown in the Mini Mind Map above.

Wherever there is a focus on a particular theme, the icon for that theme appears in the margin (see p. x for key). Look out, too, for the 'Style and language' sections. Being able to comment on style and language will help you to get an 'A' in your exam.

USE YOUR NOVEL

You will learn more from the Commentary if you use it alongside the novel itself. Read a section from the novel, then the corresponding Commentary section – or the other way round.

Remember that when a question appears in the Commentary with a star ✪ in front of it, you should stop and think about it for a moment. And **remember** to take a break after completing each exercise!

Chapter 1

Finding the plates

◆ Alison and Gwyn hear strange scratching in the loft.
◆ Gwyn finds a set of dinner plates there.

Alison is feeling unwell and uncomfortable. She has heard a scratching noise in the loft every night which has got progressively louder. She feels strange and *jittery*. ✪ Do you think there is likely to be a logical explanation for the noise? Why is Alison so disturbed by it? Gwyn insists that the noise is made by rats until he knocks on the ceiling and his knocks are answered. Look at the way he works out the practical details of how to get into the loft and isn't put off by the even louder scratching.

We can see Gwyn's sense of humour from the beginning. When the 'rats' copy the rhythm of his knocking he says they should be at the grammar school and jokes about putting these clever rats in a television show called Gwyn's Educated Rats. ✪ What kind of humour does Gwyn have? What does it tell you about him? Gwyn jokingly calls out to scare whatever is in the loft. He quotes from a poem by Walter de la Mare about a traveller who knocks at a deserted house. ✪ How do you think Gwyn would say these words? What do you think about the way he can quote from a poem in this way? Gwyn leaves a cage to trap the creatures, saying he still wants to know what kind of rats can count.

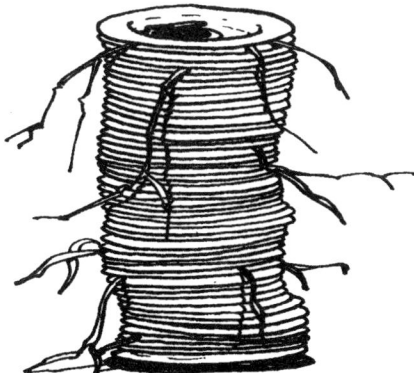

Look at the way Gwyn's mother talks to him, and the way he does what she says. ✪ What impression do you get of her character?

Think about

? Before you go on to the next chapter take 10 minutes to think about Gwyn and Alison, and the strange happenings so far. From the words listed below, circle those which best describe Gwyn, and underline those which best describe Alison.

uneasy	clever	friendly	edgy
curious	logical		nervous
practical	sensitive		determined
thoughtful	helpful		quick-witted

? Look at the odd things that happen in this chapter. Some of the incidents don't seem important at the time, but we see their significance as the novel continues. Here are some of the strange occurrences so far.

- the scratching
- the connection between the scratching and Alison
- the plates
- the smell of meadowsweet in the loft
- the heat in the loft
- Gwyn nearly falling as he picks up a plate

Begin a Mind Map showing these aspects. You could use categories like smells, sounds, events, feelings.

now take a break before Roger's strange encounter

Chapter 2

The Stone of Gronw

(To p. 14, *His bedroom was immediately below hers, on the first floor.*)

◆ Roger is swimming at the Stone of Gronw.
◆ He feels something fly past him and hears a scream.
◆ Gwyn tells Roger about the scratching and the plates in the loft.

Roger sprawls on the ground after his swim. The only things he can hear are the river and a farmer calling sheep. The mountains are described as *gentle* , and the flowers have a *cool sweet air*. Meadowsweet grows thickly round the base of the rock. ✪ Where have these flowers been mentioned before?

Suddenly Roger feels something fly past him and vibrate through the rock, and he hears a scream. He leaps up, but there is no one in sight. Notice how everything that was pleasant a minute ago is now harsh and threatening. He is cold in the heat of the sun. His skin crawls with gooseflesh, his hands are bleeding where the meadowsweet cut him, and the flowers smell pungent and unpleasant. Roger sees that the hole in the rock forms a frame through which you can look straight to the fir trees above the house. ✪ Look at Roger's thoughts about what has happened. What does he feel about the incident, and the rock?

Huw makes conversation with Roger about swimming.
❂ What do you notice about the way Huw speaks? Roger
responds briefly and curtly. He calls Huw *'gaga'* and says he's
'off his head'. ❂ What do you think of his attitude to Huw, and
the language he uses to describe him?

Gwyn describes the weird experience he had as he picked up
the first plate, as if in a second something changed. He is
surprised that Roger understands exactly what he means.
❂ What happened to Roger at the moment when Gwyn lifted
the plate? Notice the way Gwyn praises Roger's description of
that kind of moment. Notice that Roger doesn't tell Gwyn
about his experience at the rock. He is evasive when Gwyn
asks him why he wants to know about the rock.

Over to you

?   Before you go on, you could add to your Mind Map.
    Include what happened at the Stone of Gronw, and
    the details of what happened to Gwyn when he
    picked up the plate.

?   Look at what Huw said when Gwyn told him about
    the plates. Gwyn says he wasn't talking about Alison
    when he said *'Mind how you are looking at her.'* Have
    you any idea at this point what or who he means?
    Start to **make a list** of the mysterious things Huw says,
    and when he says them.

China owls

(From p. 14, *She was bending over a plate,* to p. 16, *'I must
make some more,' said Alison.*)

◆ Alison traces the design on the plate, cuts round it and
  bends it into an owl shape.
◆ She says she must make more.

Alison is absorbed in tracing the pattern on the plate.
She's impatient when Roger doesn't immediately see that
the abstract flowery design can be turned into an owl. When
she shows him, he says it's really good and asks how she
worked it out. Alison didn't have to work it out, she saw it

immediately. We see she is very protective of the paper owl and doesn't want Roger to play around with it. Alison also says the owl is female. ✪ How does she know? Notice the way she says *'I must make some more'*. ✪ What does the word 'must' suggest? Roger says the pattern can be an owl *'if you want it to be'*. As you read the book, think about whether the powerful events it describes have any connection with the characters' feelings, or are entirely outside them.

Look at the way Roger examines the plate to see if it has any value. He was interested when Gwyn said that they might be worth pounds. He's disappointed when he sees there is no maker's mark. He dismisses the plate as being ordinary and not worth much. ✪ What does this tell you about Roger? Jot down some notes on your impression of Roger so far.

A plain white plate

(From p. 16, *'I put the lettuce by the sink,'* to end of chapter.)

◆ Gwyn and Nancy argue.
◆ Gwyn tells her about the plates.
◆ Nancy demands the plate from Alison.
◆ Alison gives the plate to Nancy.
◆ The pattern has disappeared.

Nancy tells Gwyn to wash the lettuce before he goes to see Alison. ✪ What do you think Nancy feels about Gwyn being with Alison, and talking to Huw? Nancy feels that Gwyn is letting her down by talking Welsh *like a labourer.* What do you think about Nancy's attitude to the Welsh language? Nancy is not impressed by Gwyn's claim that he needs to practise Welsh for his exams. What does she feel about Gwyn being at the Grammar School?

Nancy is shaken when she hears they have found the plates, and demands the plate back from Alison. Look at how Roger leaves when Nancy and Alison begin to argue. When Nancy enters the room Alison hides the plate under her pillow. ✪ Why does she do this? Alison speaks arrogantly to Nancy when she reminds her that it is not Nancy's house. Gwyn thinks she is going to order Nancy from the room.

Nancy's response when Alison gives her the plain plate shows that she feels she has been tricked and is angry. Gwyn also thinks Alison has played a trick. ✪ Why does he give a silent whistle? What does he think about Alison's 'trick'?

STYLE AND LANGUAGE

You may have noticed the way Alan Garner describes objects and the landscape. The dinner service, for example, is conveyed visually in the **image** (word picture) *squat towers of plates.* The thickly clustered flowers round the rock are a *foam of meadowsweet* and the river is seen as *sliding like oil.* (The first phrase is a **metaphor** – a description of a thing as if it were something essentially different. The second is a **simile** – a comparison of two things which are different in most ways but similar in one important way.)

The use of adjectives and descriptive language is limited and restrained. People are hardly described at all. You may have your own ideas of what the characters look like, but they won't be based on details from the text. The writer presents his characters through actions and, most effectively, through dialogue. He captures the rhythm of speech and lets the characters reveal themselves through what they say. The effect at times is almost like reading a script. ✪ From your knowledge of the book up to this point, do you think it could be successfully adapted for television or radio? What changes would you need to make for each?

Over to you

?   Remember to add to your Mind Map. Then look at the illustration of the plate. Read the description on page 15 where Alison describes the pattern. Trace and cut out the design to make an owl.

?   Who do you find the most appealing character so far, Alison, Gwyn or Roger? Write a short paragraph explaining your choice.

more strange goings on — after the break

Chapter 3

The crack in the pebble-dash

◆ The plate incident has upset the household.
◆ The pattern on the plate has disappeared.
◆ Roger brings down more plates and Alison starts to make more owls.
◆ A crack has just appeared in the pebble-dash on the billiard-room wall.
◆ Clive tells Alison to keep Nancy happy.

The household is in turmoil. Nancy is threatening to leave and the upset has caused Alison's mother Margaret to feel faint and ill. Roger can't accept Alison's explanation that the pattern just disappeared. Look at the way he examines the glaze and searches for a logical explanation. ✪ Is this reaction typical of Roger?

Alison tells Roger about the strange experience when Gwyn first touched the plate. Roger has already heard this from Gwyn. You may remember that he seemed to understand what Gwyn was describing. ✪ Why doesn't he react to Alison's account? Notice that Alison can't find the owls she made earlier. ✪ Does Roger realise that she feels compelled to make them?

Roger is interested in what the original house was like. He thinks it's a shame that the original walls are covered with fake panelling and that part of the wall is pebble-dashed. Look at

the way Clive responds to Roger. He makes comments like
I dare say and *Fancy that*. He shows no curiosity about the
sudden crack in the pebble-dash. He offers an opinion about
the pebble-dashing – unlike Roger, he thinks it's quite tasteful.
We learn that Clive used to be 'on the road' in business.

Clive brings Alison her supper and admires the paper owls. ✪
Is he at all curious about them? Does he connect the plates in
Alison's room with the plates Nancy was *dead set against?*
Clive seems embarrassed when Alison asks if he's been sent to
tell her off. He tells Alison that it's important to keep Nancy
happy because Margaret couldn't cope if Nancy left. ✪ What
do you think of Clive's relationship with Margaret?

Alison complains that Nancy acted as if she owned the place,
and repeats that it is her house, and she shouldn't have to take
orders from her cook. The house is Alison's because her father
signed it over to her before he died. ✪ What do you think of
Alison's attitude to Nancy?

Your turn

Think about what you have discovered about Clive so far. Read
the following statements and decide whether each one is true
or false. Put a tick or a cross in the appropriate column (or a
question mark if you are unsure). You may like to leave some
for the moment, and find you change your mind about others
as you read on.

Statement	✓	✗	?
He is Alison's father.			
He enjoys playing snooker			
He enjoys fishing			
He is Margaret's first husband			
He does what Margaret says			
He is scared of Margaret			
Margaret's family approved of her marriage to Clive			
He is scared of Alison			
He is a forceful personality			
He likes a peaceful life			
He doesn't mind telling people off			
He has strong opinions			

He is a weak character
He gets his own way
He manage to calm Nancy by talking to her
He manages to calm Nancy by giving her money
He is rich because he inherited money through his family
He is rich because he has a successful business

If you have time you could use these ideas to write a paragraph about your impressions of Clive up to this point in the book.

You've already looked at the way Alan Garner uses dialogue. Think now about the way different characters may be identified by the way they speak. Clive uses vague expressions and clichés like *Fair do's* and *Fancy that*. Roger uses slang like *a right barny* and *tizz*. How is Gwyn's way of speaking different from theirs?

Begin a chart showing the typical expressions used by different characters. Add comments about what the way of speaking tells you about the character.

	Expression	**Any comment**
Roger		
Gwyn		
Alison		
Clive		
Nancy		

now that you have an understanding of the characters have a short break before reading about more mysterious events in the next chapter

Chapter 4

Disappearing owls and flying plates ◎

- ◆ The scratching continues in the loft and in Alison's room.
- ◆ The paper owls and the pattern on the other plates have disappeared.
- ◆ Nancy will stay only if the loft is nailed up.
- ◆ Gwyn, Alison and Roger plan to bring down the rest of the plates before this happens.
- ◆ A plate flies at Nancy and others hit the pebble-dashed wall.

Gwyn doesn't believe Alison's statement that she hadn't switched the plates to give Nancy a plain one, but no one can explain how the pattern has gone from the plates Roger brought down from the loft, or the disappearance of all the paper owls. Roger suggests leaving the rest of the plates in the loft. ✪ What do you think of his suggestion?

Gwyn describes how angry Nancy is. She's particularly furious at Alison's 'switching' the plates. ✪ What do you think Gwyn means when he says Nancy is talking *like a Welsh nationalist?* Notice that Nancy won't have Huw in the house and so nailing up the loft will be delayed, leaving them time to get down the rest of the plates.

Alison is insistent that they must get the other plates down because she feels compelled to make the owls from them. In her tension and frustration she bursts out with a criticism of Nancy. Look at the way Gwyn responds to this. ✪ Why does he call her *Miss Alison* at this point?

Nancy accuses Alison of throwing the plate at her out of spite and to mock her. She implies that Alison looks sweet and innocent but is different underneath. ✪ Why does she think it was Alison who threw the plate? Alison says she couldn't help it – but we know she didn't throw the plate.

Gwyn takes the blame although he knows it will mean *a clip on the earhole.* ✪ Why does he do this? Gwyn says his mother is touchy because he is going to have to talk to Huw about the loft. He will buy her cigarettes and calm her down. Look at the way he refers to her as *the old darling.*

✪ How does Gwyn feel about this incident?

The house in the valley

Roger wants to know what's going on. He seems to feel that Alison and Gwyn understand about the plates and he doesn't. He calls it a *peculiar business*. ✪ How do you think Roger views the odd experiences they are having? Gwyn looks around the billiard room for clues as to who could have broken the plates, just as he tries to work out who could have thrown the plate at Nancy.

Look at the description of the atmosphere just before the pebble-dash comes off the wall. The oak beams warmed by the sun give off a sweet smell which is a reminder of all the past years and all the past uses of this room, the old dairy. This seems to create a moment of heightened awareness, preparing us for the dramatic end of the chapter as the two eyes are revealed.

STYLE AND LANGUAGE

When Gwyn says that Nancy doesn't want Huw in the house but needs him to board up the loft, he uses the expression *hoist by her own petard*. This phrase comes from William Shakespeare's play *Hamlet,* and refers to someone being blown up by his own bombing device. ✪ Is it typical of Gwyn to quote like this? Does anyone else in the novel use language in this way? You could add this example to your chart.

Think about

? Take 10 minutes to think about Nancy. You could make a Mind Map. Here are two questions you might ask about her. Try to think of some more.

- Why doesn't Nancy want Gwyn to talk to Huw?
- Why is Nancy so against Alison?

? You could use what you have read so far and the notes you have made and write a few lines about Nancy's relationship with Gwyn, Alison and Huw.

? Add to your list of questions about Nancy as you go through the book.

time for a break, before reading about Roger's bright idea

Chapter 5

'Come, apple-sweet murmurer'

- Roger shows Clive the Stone of Gronw.
- Gwyn feels a disturbance in the sky.
- Huw speaks mysteriously about a woman who is coming.
- Huw tells Gwyn the plates came from his grandfather.
- He tells them the story of how Gronw was killed.
- Gwyn shows Alison and Roger what has happened in the billiard-room.

Clive assumes Nancy just made a mistake about someone throwing the plate at her. Look at the way both Roger and Clive think that Gwyn made a good move in taking the blame. When Clive says the view through the hole in the rock is like a snapshot, Roger gets the idea of taking a photograph through it. ✪ How do Clive and Roger get on? Why does Roger want to take a photograph?

Huw tells Gwyn that his grandfather used to work in the house, and was said to have gone mad in the wood in the garden. The house has always been lived in by English visitors, according to Huw, and the owners at the time sacked his grandfather, who was forced to leave the valley. He decorated the plates and sent them to the house.

Clive is interested in the hole in the rock, but he isn't at all intrigued by the story. He says it was *a bit off* to take someone else's wife, and that the revenge was *tit for tat*. He refers to *these old yarns*. Notice Roger's response. He is scornful of Huw and calls him an old liar, and refers to the husband in the story as a *stiff*. He laughs off the strange feeling he had at the stone. ✪ Who ridicules the story more, Clive or Roger? Can you think why this might be?

Gwyn points out that everything has changed since he picked up the plate. As he picked it up he felt a kind of shock, and at the same time Roger felt the vibration and scream at the Stone.

STYLE AND LANGUAGE

The sky is so strange that it makes Gwyn's heart shake. Words like *throbbed, flashed, pulse* and *trembling* give an impression of movement and expectancy. Huw's chanting increases the sense that something is going to happen. ❂ What do you think of the phrases *apple-sweet murmurer* and *harp of my gladness*? Where are they likely to come from?

Over to you

You can see now that the odd happenings in the house have some connection with the past. Before you go on, turn back to page 1 and read the account of the legend to which Huw refers. **Remember** to add to your chart showing Huw's mysterious sayings. You have also got some good examples in this chapter of the way people speak. Look at the way Clive responds to the legend, for example. How does Clive feel about strong emotions such as passion and jealousy?

have a break before finding out what they discover in the billiard-room

Chapter 6

Owls and flowers

◆ A life-size oil-painting of a woman is revealed behind the pebble-dash.
◆ Gwyn gets the rest of the plates down from the loft.
◆ He finds an owl pellet in the cage.

Notice the different attitudes the three of them have to the painting. Alison thinks she's beautiful and can't understand why anyone would want to cover her up. Roger assesses how old the painting is, marvels at its condition and is excited at the thought of how much money they will get for it. Gwyn says they have to keep quiet about it. He has thought about how the mysterious events are connected to each other.

He points out to them that someone cared enough to cover up the painting and hide the plates. He says his mother is scared stiff and would take an axe to the painting if she saw it. He reminds them of Huw's references to a woman.

As Gwyn says, the weather is called *she* in Welsh. ✪ Do you think Huw could be talking about the weather? Why does Roger think that he is? Notice that Roger doesn't want them to get the other plates down. ✪ Has he said this before? Why is he getting *cold feet*?

Gwyn notices that the clover petals are in fact fine, sharp claws. He sees a connection between owls and flowers and feels that it is dangerous. He senses that there will be trouble now that the plates and the painting are released from their hiding places. Gwyn feels that Alison is at the centre. He says she must be *disconnected* in the same way as you stop a battery working by removing the wires.

STYLE AND LANGUAGE

You have already looked at some of the language used in the previous chapter to describe the strange, vibrant sky. The air is said to flash *like blue lightning*. Gwyn also describes it as being like *strip lighting switched on*. Now, he uses an image of batteries and wires. ✪ What do you find is the effect of these images of energy and electricity?

Think about

? Stop for 10 minutes and concentrate on Alison. What do you think of her? Make a Mind Map of the important things she does and says. By now you should be building up a picture of Alison in your mind. **Remember** to add to your Mind Map as you read the rest of the book.

now that you're getting a clear idea of Alison's character, take a break

Chapter 7

Going to the shop

◆ Nancy refuses to give Gwyn his pocket money in advance.
◆ Gwyn puts the owl pellet in Nancy's purse.
◆ Roger goes to the shop with him.
◆ The women in the shop talk in Welsh about Huw, owls, and a woman coming.
◆ Alison denies knowledge of the plates.

Look at the way Gwyn asks for his pocket money. ❷ Do you think he is cheeky to Nancy? Roger is uneasy when he thinks Gwyn is taking the money from Nancy's purse. He tries to make it all right in his own mind by saying that Gwyn is just *anticipating* his allowance. ❷ What does this tell you about Roger? He is very shaken when Gwyn puts the pellet in her purse. He says, *'After all, she is your mother.'* ✪ How is Roger and Clive's relationship different from Gwyn and Nancy's? Roger offers to lend Gwyn the money, and says he can put the cigarettes on the house's account. ✪ What does Gwyn feel about Roger's offer? Gwyn's reference to the owl pellet as *a poor thing, but mine own* is another quotation from a Shakespeare play.

Notice how the talk in the shop is a mixture of everyday language to do with household goods and mysterious expressions like the ones Huw uses. The women say that Huw has been round to all the farms warning them that *she is coming* and *this time it's owls*, because that's what Alison has made. ✪ To whom do you think they are referring? If it's owls this time, what might it have been another time? What other pattern could Alison have chosen from the plates? The women talk as if they fear what is going to happen, but can't escape from it. ✪ Why do you think they switch from English to Welsh when the boys go in? Why doesn't Gwyn tell Roger what they were talking about?

Try this

Look at the triangle here. One corner is filled in. Decide whose names should go at each of the other points, and write them in.

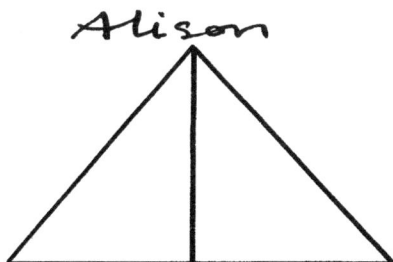

Alison

have a break before going on to read more about the happenings of long ago in the valley!

Chapter 8

The *Mabinogion*

◆ Alison is reading a collection of Welsh myths.
◆ Gwyn and Alison argue.
◆ Gwyn kicks her book.
◆ The book flies at him.
◆ They discuss the story of Lleu, Gronw and the woman of flowers.

When Gwyn asks Alison where the plates are she replies in a very haughty manner. She criticises the way he speaks. ✪ Why does Alison say Gwyn is just like his mother? What do you think of her saying this?

The book flies towards Gwyn. ✪ What do you think causes this to happen? What does it remind you of? Look at the way the trees seem to attack him and the bag of flour hits him as he runs to the wood.

The tension between Gwyn and Alison disappears as the three of them piece together the torn pages of the book, and Alison apologises when she hears the book belongs to one of Gwyn's teachers. Gwyn jokes that the pieces of paper look like confetti.

The pages they piece together tell the story of Blodeuwedd, Lleu and Gronw (see 'Background' p. 1).

✪ Think about the plates in the loft. How does the pattern on them relate to the old story? Look at the way the three of them react to the story. Roger recognises that they are actually in the place where these events occurred, but he jokes about it. He says it's like the Ku Klux Klan, a secret society in the southern states of America (he probably thinks the name sounds like Lleu Llaw Gyffes), and sarcastically calls Huw *Professor*. He uses the Welsh pronunciation of 'Ll' as 'Cl' to make a pun, a play on words, based on 'Lleu' and 'clue'. ✪ Why does Roger behave in this way? Which of them sees the connection with the plates?

Think about

? Use your ideas about the connections between the ancient legend and the strange happenings in the valley at the moment to add to your Mind Map of the mysterious event.

? Here is another triangle. Blodeuwedd's name is at the top. Decide which names should go at the other two points and write them in.

Blodeuwedd

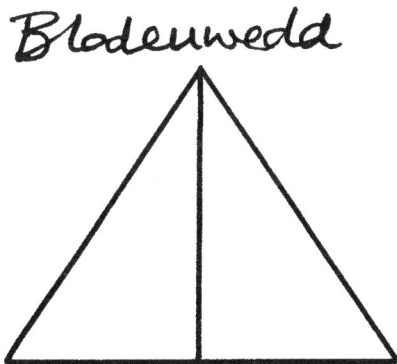

? Look at the description of the book flying at Gwyn and him blundering across the wood away from it. Words like *swarmed, spun, whipping* and *smacked* create an impression of force and even violence. Think about the other places in the book when you have been aware of powerful forces.

? On p. 43 Gwyn uses an unusual word: **axiomatic**. You've already looked at some aspects of Gwyn's use of language and should have been entering them in your language chart. On the next page is a list of some of the unusual words Gwyn uses and a list of meanings. Match the words with the meanings and check your answers in a dictionary.

Words	Meanings
axiomatic (p. 43)	lacking in good manners
elliptical (p.75)	altered from its original structure
uncouth (p. 58)	obscure, not clear
metamorphic (p. 90)	containing a general truth

now you've improved your word-power, time for some photography — after the break!

Chapter 9

'You think it's haunted, then?'

(To p. 51, and the shadows seemed to come out of the river.)

◆ Clive buys Alison an owl made of shells.
◆ Gwyn searches for the plates.
◆ They hear movement in the room above the stables.
◆ Gwyn asks Roger about his mother.
◆ Roger takes photographs through the hole in the Stone of Gronw.

Clive comes back from shopping with the film for Roger (the wrong one) and a shell owl for Alison. Gwyn is sure Alison has hidden the plates as he has searched everywhere for them. He and Roger try to see if she is in the locked stable room and decide the swishing noise might be dead leaves. Roger is very disturbed by the noise he heard the night before in Alison's room. He knows something is wrong but isn't convinced by Gwyn's list of odd happenings. Roger looks for logical explanations and won't follow up the connection with the *Mabinogion*. He concentrates instead on taking the photograph.

Notice that Gwyn seems to have instinctive knowledge of the valley, maybe formed by his mother's talk about it. We find out here that Nancy started work in the kitchen of the house when she was 12. ❷ How might this affect the way she sees the house and its new owner? Gwyn talks about the effect it has on the community when people from England pay high rents for holiday homes in Wales. Gwyn gets very excited when he recognises a connection between the plates and one of Huw's sayings. ❂ What is the connection?

Look at the way Roger threatens to hit Gwyn if he asks any more about his real mother. ❂ Why do you think he reacts like this?

Gold saddles and gold bridles

(From p. 51, *'Taking photos, are you?'* to end.)

◆ Huw finds Roger taking the photograph.
◆ Huw says he made horses and greyhounds out of toadstools.

Roger is sarcastic to Huw when he asks what Roger is photographing, and he tries to get rid of him. He's impatient when Huw refers to the legend, but does listen when Huw talks about Lleu's hurt and pride and loss. Roger has in fact thought about the story. He thinks Gronw had guts, and he doesn't support Blodeuwedd's behaviour. Huw says that individually they weren't to blame, but together they destroyed each other.

Huw tells Roger that he got his nickname because when they were short of bacon in the valley he got some pigs in exchange for 12 fine horses and greyhounds, which he made out of toadstools. Roger is convinced that Huw is mad.

Have a go at this

Stop for 10 minutes or so and jot down your own thoughts about the old legend. You could do this in a Mind Map. Huw appears to see all sides of the story and to understand the characters' feelings. Look at the statements below and make up your own mind as to whether each character is to blame or not. Depending on what you decide, put either a tick or a cross at the end of each statement. If you are unsure, put a question mark.

Lleu

His mother was hostile to him and placed curses on him.
One curse was that he couldn't have a mortal wife.
He could only have a wife made out of flowers.
His wife is unfaithful to him.

His wife and her lover Gronw conspire to kill him.
They fail to kill him because the magician Gwydion saves him.
Lleu kills Gronw.

Gronw
He falls in love with Blodeuwedd.
His rival Lleu has magical protection.
He thinks he has killed Lleu.
He lives happily with Blodeuwedd.
Gronw asks what 'blood payment' Lleu will take.
Lleu claims the right to throw the spear at Gronw
in return.
Gronw accepts this and is killed.

Blodeuwedd
She is not mortal.
As soon as she is created she is married to Lleu.
She may long to be flowers on the mountain again.
She falls in love with Gronw.
She helps Gronw to 'kill' Lleu.
She is punished by being turned into an owl.
She is condemned by other birds and hunts alone at night.

take a quick break before the next chapter

Chapter 10

'I shouldn't have come'

◆ Clive tells Gwyn off for writing a note to Alison.
◆ Roger complains to Clive about Huw.
◆ Alison ignores Gwyn's signal that he wants to talk to her.
◆ Gwyn and Nancy talk about Huw.

Gwyn makes the sitting-room comfortable for Clive and Roger. ✪ What details make you aware of Gwyn's *servant* status? Look at the way Gwyn reacts when Clive tells him off for leaving the note for Alison. ✪ What do you think Gwyn feels at this point?

Roger complains that Huw was trying to louse up his photograph. He calls him a *moron* and a *real nutter*. Clive says they can't get rid of Huw. ✪ What reasons does he give? What do you think is the most important reason for Clive?

Look at the way Alison ignores Gwyn's signal. ✪ Why does she do this?

Nancy is upset and close to tears. She took the job in the house for the money and now wishes she hadn't. ✪ Who gave Margaret Nancy's address? Look at the way Nancy won't talk about Huw. She says he is an idiot and doesn't count, but Gwyn senses that Huw is an important person in the valley. He knows there is a connection with the plates. We can see how strongly Nancy feels when she says that if Gwyn talks about it any more she will make him leave school and work behind the Co-op counter. Nancy seems to think that Gwyn's education will cause him to look down on her as the family in the house do. She is also afraid that Gwyn has been listening to talk about her in the valley. ✪ What do you think of her threat to take Gwyn away from school?

Think about Gwyn's response to Nancy's threat. ✪ What does he feel about it? Look at what he says when Nancy needs an aspirin. First, he corrects her grammar. ✪ Why does Gwyn choose this particular 'put-down', do you think? He then suggests that she looks in her purse. ✪ What has he put in her purse? What are Gwyn's feelings for Nancy at this point?

Your turn

Before you go on to the next chapter you might like to add to the list of questions or Mind Map about Nancy that you started earlier.

Look at Gwyn's behaviour in this chapter. Jot down the places where you feel sympathy for him. You could begin a Mind Map of Gwyn if you haven't already done so.

give yourself a break, and prepare for some very strange happenings in the next chapter!

Chapter 11

Gwyn follows Alison

(To p. 64, *Got you.*)

◆ Gwyn keeps watch on Alison.
◆ When the family are asleep she slips out through the cloakroom door.
◆ He follows her into the marshy wood.
◆ He is surrounded by flames and is terrified, then realises the flames are marsh gas.

We see Gwyn working out what Alison's likely movements will be. Notice that he has already been standing for two hours without moving. ✪ What does this tell you about Gwyn? Look at the way he concentrates on the separate elements and the specific types of sound he can hear. We are also told that he plays with time, splitting it and compressing it, to help him wait. ✪ How does the novel as a whole play with time? Is there a clear distinction between the past and the present? One of the sounds Gwyn hears is a motorcycle. ✪ Has this been heard before?

Gwyn seems to be involved in a kind of competition with Alison. He doesn't want her to get the better of him. Look at the way he says, *'Now let's see how good you really are'* when he thinks she might try to slip out of the house too soon, then admits she's *not bad at all* when she waits for an hour before leaving.

Gwyn loses sight of Alison, then works out that she must be in the wood. He can't work out what Alison is up to as her light goes on and off and he tries to follow her movements, puzzling about how she can move so quickly. Gwyn wonders if Alison knows he is there and is trying to give him the slip. He sees it as a game, a contest between him and Alison, and begins to enjoy it. ✪ What do you think about the way he thinks of Alison as *girlie* and *Miss Alison* in this chapter?

Look at the way Gwyn is suddenly surrounded by flames. The short sharp sentences convey his feeling of panic. He feels trapped and useless, cut off from the world outside and imprisoned in this wood where Huw's father went mad. He tries to keep himself sane by repeating rules of physics and spelling, chemistry and history, hanging on to known facts to protect himself from the unknown. This strategy leads him to remember that a gas composed mainly of methane is produced when vegetation decomposes under water, and forms the kind of flame he is seeing. Gwyn laughs in relief when he realises he has been scared of marsh gas. Then he becomes angry with himself for panicking. He imagines Alison laughing at him as she tells Roger how he screamed at the top of his voice and she gave him the slip. Look at the way he insults himself. ✪ Why does he include *Welsh git* in his list of abusive terms?

'She's come'

(From p. 64, *She was standing under a tree*, to end of chapter.)

◆ Gwyn realises the figure he's been watching is not Alison.
◆ He finds Alison in an old hen hut, with the plates, cutting out owls.
◆ Alison and Gwyn talk about her need to make the owls and her power to move objects.
◆ Huw says that *she* has come.

Gwyn thinks he sees Alison at the end of the causeway. He watches her movements and determines to follow her when she thinks she's safe. He hears a sneeze from the direction of the hut and realises the figure he has been watching can't be Alison. As he watches the figure disappears. ✪ Who do you think the figure could be?

Gwyn hears strange noises coming from the hut: a fluttering like wings and a ruffling of the plates. We see him bursting into the hut and throwing himself on Alison to stop her making the owls. Alison describes what it's like when she feels the compulsion to make the owls building up inside her. She feels strung up and edgy, as if she's going to burst. When Gwyn asks her how she made the plate fly at Nancy and the book fly at him, she does not seem to realise that she is responsible. She just feels the same sensations as when she needs to make the owls.

Alison tells Gwyn how frightened she is. She feels that time has become confused so that she can't distinguish between past, present and future. Her feelings are confused as well.

Look at the way Gwyn tries to calm her down. ✪ What do you think of his tactics?

When Gwyn tries to take Alison back to the house she refuses to go past the marsh gas. She accepts Gwyn's explanation that it is just a compound of carbon and hydrogen, but says that it is being used. ✪ Do you think the marsh gas is just a natural occurrence, or do you think its appearance at this point could be another example of the strange powers at work? Gwyn stays with Alison until dawn. As they go back to the house Huw is raking the drive, although it is only four in the morning.

STYLE AND LANGUAGE

This chapter is very tense and atmospheric. You should have already noticed the use of short sharp sentences to create a sense of panic. Garner adds to this in his presentation of Gwyn's thoughts, which are woven into the narrative. As Gwyn waits for Alison to move we are told *The light was steady*, and this is immediately followed by Gwyn's thought: *Your move, old stick.* ✪ Find some more examples of this technique, and notice how it adds to the dramatic tension.

Look also at the description of the marshy wood on p. 61. We have a strong sense of the ancient land in the repetition of the word *old*, and can feel the way this land is turning back to swamp when Gwyn can't steady himself because the trees *heeled over* with *their roots adrift*. Throughout the chapter words like *slime*, *rotten* and *rotting* add to the impression of decaying and shifting ground.

You might have noticed the powerful **simile** used to describe the fluttering sound Gwyn hears in the hut. It is said to be *like wings, but dry and hard as a rattlesnake.* ✪ How does this image create a sense of danger? What do you associate with a rattlesnake?

More for you to do

?   Stop for 10 minutes and think about Alison and Gwyn. Huw says *'She's come'*. Alison has now finished making the owls of the whole dinner service. Think about the connections between Alison and the owls, the painting of the woman covered in flowers, and the story of Blodeuwedd. Add to your Mind Map of Alison.

? Look at the way Gwyn's feelings for Alison change during this chapter. What does he think and feel as he follows her? How does he respond when Alison tell him she's frightened? Add to your Mind Map of Gwyn.

you've earned a break — before reading about a power set loose in the valley

Chapter 12

'She wants to be flowers, but you make her owls'

◆ Gwyn questions Huw about the plates.
◆ Huw says his grandfather saw the lady made of flowers in the wood.
◆ Huw says the lady wants to be made of flowers, but is being made of owls.
◆ He speaks of a power which is set free in the valley.
◆ Huw and his ancestors cannot free themselves from these ancient happenings.

Gwyn kicks away Huw's rake so that he falls over and challenges him about why he is raking the drive at this hour of the morning. ✪ What is Gwyn feeling? What does he mean when he says Huw can fool the others but not him?

In answer to Gwyn's questions, Huw says that Blodeuwedd is the lady and that she has come. She is the same lady his grandfather saw in the wood. Gwyn goes pale when he hears this. ✪ How does he know the exact spot where she appeared? Remember what happened to him as he was following Alison. Look at the way Huw grabs and hurts Gwyn as he insists that he should not go to that place. He seems to include Gwyn in the references to his family.

Gwyn desperately tries to understand Huw's mysterious answers, but Huw says that Gwyn does know the truth. He talks about the three, Lleu, Gronw and Blodeuwedd. He says the power of the valley is contained within them and set free through them. These three suffer every time. ✪ Think about the triangles you drew. Who are the three who will suffer now?

Huw says that the unhappy spirit of Blodeuwedd brought sorrow to the valley in the time of his grandfather and his uncle. They tried to calm her, but they *made her owls*. ✪ What do you think Blodeuwedd wants to be? They thought they had tamed her by capturing her on the plates and in the painting. Huw suggests that the trouble is passed down through the generations of his family because of the wrongs that were done in the first place. One wrong was to use the natural powers of flowers and make them into a thinking person.

Huw is muddled about who made the woman and who painted the plates. The person who actually made the woman of flowers was a magician called Gwydion. ✪ Can you remember a place earlier in the book where Huw described himself playing a magic trick?

Gwyn says Huw has to straighten himself out. He sees that Huw is frightened and he feels fear himself. He tries to warn Huw that the family at the house think he's off his head, and Roger is trying to get him sacked. Gwyn thinks that Huw puts on an act, pretending to be a daft old servant, to add a bit of local colour. He reminds Huw that he doesn't own the place. ✪ What do you think about Huw's reply?

A quick exercise

Go back to your list of the strange things Huw says. You may like to add some of the material from this chapter. Do you find that his mysterious comments begin to make sense?

Jot down what the different characters (Gwyn, Roger, Clive and Nancy) think of Huw.

now you have a clearer idea of the connection between owls and flowers, and the pattern on the plates – take a break

Chapter 13

'Mummy said I wasn't to talk to you' ◎

◆ Alison defies her mother and meets Gwyn near the hen house.

◆ She tells Gwyn her father inherited the house from a cousin called Bertram.

◆ Roger reminds Alison that she has been forbidden to speak to Gwyn.

Clive shows concern over Alison's peaky appearance the morning after the night in the hut. He reminds her of an instruction from Margaret. Notice how he supports Margaret, explaining that she has Alison's best interests at heart and wants her to enjoy herself. ✪ Do you think Clive agrees with Margaret?

Alison tells Gwyn that she doesn't feel as if she belongs in the valley even though she's spent holidays at the house all her life. She points out that Gwyn seems to have a deep knowledge of the place, as if he'd always lived there. Gwyn asks Alison how much say she has in the running of the house and the estate, since it does belong to her. We hear that Alison's father inherited the house from his cousin Bertram, who was killed years ago. Gwyn hopes that Alison can use her position as owner to save Huw's job. Gwyn is sorry that he lost his temper with him, and thinks that Huw may be talking sense after all.

Alison tells Gwyn he's the only one she can talk to, and that she couldn't help ignoring him the other day because her mother was putting a lot of pressure on her. Alison says she had no idea her mother could be so harsh. ✪ Why is Margaret so against Gwyn? Gwyn also says that he can talk to Alison. Look at the way he tries to calm her and apologises for being thoughtless when she becomes a little hysterical about the plates. ✪ What does Gwyn feel about Alison at this point?

Look at the little battle between Gwyn and Roger when Roger wants Alison to go and see his prints. ✪ What does Roger say to break up the conversation between Alison and Gwyn? Gwyn replies by calling her *Miss Alison* and saying he will use the tradesman's entrance in future. ✪ Why does Gwyn emphasise his role of servant here? How do you think he and Alison feel as he walks away?

Think about

Before you go on to the next chapter stop and think about Margaret. Although we never meet her she is a powerful character who affects the action and has an important role. Make a list or Mind Map of what you have found out about her through what you gather and what other people say. Here are a few items to start you off:

- Margaret is Alison's mother.
- Margaret is upset by Alison's treatment of Nancy.
- Margaret doesn't want Alison to associate with Gwyn.

you are now about half-way through the book – have a rest before continuing!

Chapter 14

Nancy moves the photographs

(To p. 79, *'What's this, a wet weekend in Brum?'*)

◆ Roger has laid out his prints to dry on the dining room table.
◆ He is angry with Nancy for moving them.
◆ Clive has to keep the peace.

The photographs Roger took when Huw was watching contain something strange. ✪ Why is Roger so rude about Huw?

When Nancy tells Roger she moved them because they were in the way he accuses her of interfering and says it isn't her job to make that kind of decision. ✪ What do you think of Roger's behaviour to Nancy? Clive sorts out the situation. He gets Roger to take his prints into another room, gives Nancy some money to calm her down and stop her handing in her notice, and advises Roger to *bend with the wind*. ✪ What does Clive mean by this? Why does he keep calming Nancy down?

Roger realises the prints aren't spoilt and he apologises to Clive. ✪ Do you think he should apologise to Nancy?

Clive says that Nancy wouldn't think about whether the prints were important. He refers to *the Nancys of this world*. It is typical of Clive to use this kind of generalisation. ✪ Why does he dismiss Nancy as being not very bright? Look at his comments about Gwyn. He agrees with Roger that Gwyn is smart, but says that brains aren't enough. He likens Gwyn to *barrack room lawyers* he knew in the Royal Air Force, referring to people who weren't of the same status as officers but who used their knowledge and brains to give advice and state opinions. Clive thinks that brains aren't enough without the right social background. Roger's response suggests that Margaret has been impressing this idea on Alison. ✪ What do you think of Clive's views?

The prints and the painting

(From p. 79, *'You tell me', said Roger*, to end of chapter.)

◆ Roger and Clive examine the photographs.
◆ There is a strange shape in two of them.
◆ The painting has been scraped off the wall.
◆ Roger accuses Gwyn of doing it.

Roger explains to Clive that he took a series of shots of the Stone of Gronw, making the hole frame the trees on the Bryn. He asks Clive what he sees in the last two. ✪ Why does Roger want Clive to have a look?

At first Clive thinks the extra shape in the first print is someone on a horse or pony, maybe lifting up a pole. He seems to have long hair gathered at the back. In the second enlargement the pony seems more like a motorbike. Roger thinks it was Huw's presence that made the last two photographs turn out like this. ✪ Who does the figure on the horse remind you of? Clive thinks he has a pole in his hand. What else might it be? Think about the figure on the motorbike. You may remember that the sound of a motorbike has been heard a couple of times. Clive tries to come up with rational explanations. He thinks about beatniks and motorbike scrambles, and although he isn't satisfied with these explanations, he doesn't probe any further. ✪ What do you think Roger wants Clive to say? Clive jokes that Huw has put a jinx on Roger. ✪ How does Roger respond?

Looking through the Stone of Gronw

Look at the way Clive speaks to Gwyn. ✪ How can you tell that he becomes increasingly impatient? Gwyn says 'Yes, sir' and 'At once, sir'. ✪ Why doesn't Gwyn hurry? Clive says that Gwyn is displaying *Dumb Insolence*. This phrase refers to someone who shows disrespect without actually using disrespectful words, and is a term Clive may well have used in the RAF. ✪ How does Clive think Gwyn should behave towards him?

Roger assumes that Gwyn scraped the painting off the wall. He says Gwyn is a *vindictive beggar*, suggesting that Gwyn has done it to get his own back. He orders Gwyn, '*Come here!*' and calls him a *Welsh oaf*. ✪ What do you think of the way Roger speaks to Gwyn? What does Roger think of the Welsh? You may remember that Gwyn called himself a *Welsh git*, and when he answers Roger, he assumes a mock-Welsh way of speaking, using phrases like *look you*. ✪ What point is Gwyn making by speaking like this, and by calling Roger *Master Roger*?

Now try this

❓ Remember to add the incident with the photographs to your Mind Map of mysterious events. You will also find material in this chapter to add to your language chart.

❓ When you've done that, spend a few minutes thinking about Gwyn and Roger. What do they feel about each other? Is it a straightforward relationship? Jot down or Mind Map some of the ways in which they are similar to each other and some of the ways in which they are different. Think about the way each of them sees Alison, and what we know about the relationship of each with his mother.

❓ Remember to add to your Mind Map of all the characters and their interrelationships.

time for a break, before tensions mount in Chapter 15

Chapter 15

My Mr Bertram

◆ Alison watches Gwyn through the window.
◆ She looks at her reflection in the fish tank.
◆ She sees Gwyn touch her reflection in the water.
◆ Nancy says she should have married Bertram.

Gwyn fights his anger as he takes the broken pebble-dash to the rubbish dump. We sense his rage and tension in his hunched shoulders and the way he kicks the pebbles as he walks.

Clive has said that Gwyn is not to serve the food at their meal today. Notice that Nancy says it's a pity that Gwyn didn't hit Roger. ○ Why does she feel like this? What does Gwyn imply about Roger and Clive when he says *'Daddy broke it up'*?

We see Gwyn gathering cigarettes from all over the house and giving them to Nancy as a present. He also apologises for the trick with the owl pellet. ○ Why is Gwyn behaving like this? Nancy speaks very scornfully about Roger and Clive. She resents the way Roger spoke to her about the photos, and the way Clive thinks he can make matters right by flashing his money around. She shows contempt for Clive when she says that he's not a real *gentleman*. She tests his knowledge of etiquette by serving pears with knives and forks to eat them. Nancy says that Alison covered up for Clive, but that she knew what Nancy was up to. Alison knew the *correct* way to eat the pear. ○ What does this suggest about Clive's social background, and Margaret's and Alison's? Do you think it's important to be aware of conventions such as table manners?

Nancy talks about Bertram, who she says was a real gentleman. You may remember that Bertram is the name of the cousin who owned the house until he was killed and it passed to Alison's father. We find out here that Bertram and Nancy planned to marry. He gave her the dinner plates to use when they were married. Remember that Nancy was a servant in the house. ○ What would her position have been if she had married Bertram? Notice the suggestions of opposition to their proposed marriage in Bertram's comments *'Let them think what they like'* and *'Hang the lot of them'*. ○ Who would have opposed the marriage?

Nancy feels that Bertram's death robbed her of her rightful place. She implies that it may not have been an accident, and refers to that *'jealous idiot outside'*. ○ Who does she mean?

Test yourself

? Before you go on, turn back to the list of questions you asked about Nancy. You may be able to answer some of them now. For example, you may have some more ideas about why she is resentful of the family in the house, and about her connection with the plates.

? Look at the new triangle. Write in at least one of the other names.

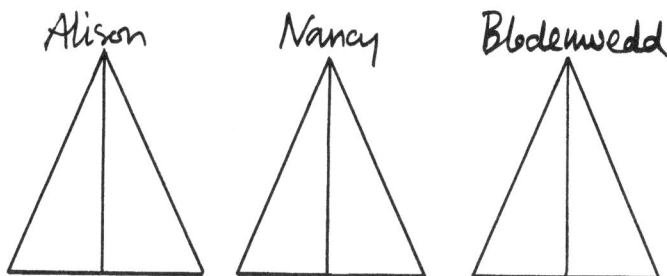

now have a short break before continuing

*C*hapter 16

Alison and Gwyn

(To p. 94, *'Come along and I'll show you.'*)

◆ Clive, Roger and Alison are at the river – Clive fishing, Roger taking photographs.
◆ Alison wants to climb the peat road up the mountain.
◆ Gwyn overhears her plan and races to get there before her.
◆ They discuss their futures, and the reflection in the fish tank that morning.

Roger still insists that Gwyn spoilt the painting out of spite, and Alison says he's wrong. She's impatient with Roger's photography and wants to go up the mountain. Roger says she's not interested in his prints. ✪ What do you think he feels about this? We see Alison passing on what she has learnt from Gwyn about the peat road. ✪ Why does she let them think she has known about this for a long time?

Alison feels scared when she climbs up out of sight. She has a strong sense of the timelessness of the valley and looks for signs of the present day for reassurance. Gwyn's appearance startles her. He laughs at her fear – but notice that his jokes about bows and arrows and woad show awareness of her state of mind.

Alison tells Gwyn that she's not allowed to talk to him or be with him. When he jokes about the situation she says she's going home, but Gwyn says he'll go with her. He wants Alison to be herself *for a change*. Alison seems to be very influenced by her mother's wishes, and says she hates upsetting her. Look at how Gwyn responds to this. ❂ What does he seem to think of Margaret? We have another example of Margaret's influence when Alison says her mother wants her to go abroad for a year when she leaves school. When Gwyn asks Alison what she herself wants to do, Alison says she hasn't thought about it, but will probably go abroad. She says that Roger will probably join Clive's business. Gwyn is very sarcastic about their plans for their future. He speaks scathingly of Alison sitting at home and arranging flowers for Mummy, and mockingly compares Alison and Roger to greyhounds straining to get away. (Remember Huw's mention of greyhounds in Chapter 9.) Then he says he doesn't blame Alison for her attitude. ❂ What does Gwyn feel about the lives that Alison and Roger expect to lead? What do you think about it?

Gwyn's teachers want him to carry on with his education, but his mother wants him to leave school and work behind a shop counter. Nancy feels that if Gwyn gets a non-manual job he will have done better than the other boys on their street. Alison seems to be quite shaken when she hears this. She realises that her life has been easy by comparison.

Notice that Gwyn tells Alison he feels he has to get out of Wales, and that he has made plans for what to do if Nancy makes him leave school. ❂ What does Gwyn feel about being Welsh? What do you think about Margaret's ambitions for Alison and Nancy's for Gwyn? How are they different and how are they similar?

When Gwyn and Alison talk about seeing Alison's reflection in the fish tank, Gwyn applies what he has learnt in physics about images and angles, and points out that what he saw in the water can't have been Alison's likeness. Gwyn says that the image in the water wasn't Alison, but was Blodeuwedd, the woman in the picture. Look at the way Alison reacts to this. She is very scared, and asks Gwyn for help. He tell her she has to face up to what is happening and stop trying to deny it. ✪ Do you sympathise with Alison?

Try this

Here is an outline map of the valley. Fill in the names of important places. You could use colour and your own illustrations, signs and symbols to link events and places. Add to it as you go through the book. Some of the places you could include are: the Bryn; the Stone of Gronw; the Ravenstone; the oak tree; the Black Hiding; the house; the shop; the river.

On the Ravenstone

(From p. 94, *Gwyn set off across the plateau* to end of chapter.)

◆ Gwyn leads Alison towards the Ravenstone, a rock at the edge of the valley.
◆ Alison tells Gwyn about Roger's mother.
◆ Gwyn teases Alison and she forgets her fear.
◆ Gwyn gets Alison to listen to the river, the last sound Lleu and Gronw heard before they died.

Gwyn and Alison understand each other. Look at the way Gwyn replies when Alison asks him if he scraped the painting off the wall. The combination of Gwyn's familiar and comforting presence and the hugeness of the landscape helps Alison to laugh and forget her fear for the moment.

Alison tells Gwyn that Roger's mother walked out on Clive and Roger. Alison's mother has told her that there was some scandal involved, and that the newspapers at the time were full of it. She has a nickname for Roger's mother: the Birmingham Belle. ✪ What does this nickname imply about Roger's mother? What does Margaret seem to think of her? We hear that Margaret doesn't use this expression in front of Roger – at least, not on purpose.

Gwyn tells Alison a story about the sheep that are bred on that side of the mountain. He says that some are bred with short left legs and some are bred with short right legs, and they have special stilts for when they are on level ground. He tells Alison the name for the stilts, which used to be carved out of wood by Welsh craftsmen, but are now made of fibre-glass. ✪ Does Gwyn's story sound convincing? Why does the joke work so well on Alison? Alison laughs as much as Gwyn when she realises she's fallen for it. Look at the way she begs him not to tell anyone else, and says that she would have felt very differently if it had been someone other than Gwyn who had made a fool of her like that. ✪ What does this tell you about her relationship with Gwyn? When Alison gets scared again when she thinks about the owls, Gwyn calms her, pointing out that they've had a good laugh and they're on top of the mountain in the sunshine.

We get a strong sense here of the way past and present merge. Gwyn gets Alison to listen to how close the river sounds, even though it's so far away. He talks about the never-ending sound of the water which was heard by Lleu and Gronw and is being heard by Gwyn and Alison now. Another sound Gwyn hears is the noise of a motorbike. You have probably noted this sound on your Mind Map of mysterious happenings. ✪ Does it suggest anything to you yet?

Over to you

Look at Gwyn's remark: *'The three of us are lame ducks'*. This suggests that Gwyn and Alison and Roger are in some way weak or vulnerable. From what you have read so far, jot down your ideas about this on the chart. A couple of suggestions have been entered.

	Source of strength	**Source of weakness/ vulnerability**
Gwyn		feelings about being Welsh
Alison		
Roger		feelings for his mother

Gwyn and Alison's relationship is getting stronger all the time — have a short rest before going on!

Chapter 17

Records that teach you to speak properly

◆ Gwyn and Alison talk about the power in the valley.
◆ They arrange to meet secretly every day in the kitchen garden.
◆ Gwyn tells Alison he has bought elocution lessons on record.
◆ Alison gives Gwyn the shell owl.

Gwyn understands that the power used to make the woman of flowers is forever contained within the valley, and builds up until it has to be let loose. There is the sense that this must happen to restore the valley to health. Huw is trying to deal with it. ✪ Why is Huw an important figure in the valley? Look at the way Gwyn describes the power, likening it to an electric plug, and wondering which of them is the earth wire. (In present-day wiring, the blue wire is neutral, the green is live and the brown is earth.) ✪ Is this an effective image?

Alison says *'I can understand how she feels always alone. No wonder she's cruel.'* ✪ Who is Alison talking about? Why does she understand her so well?

Alison feels there is some tragic mystery about Bertram. ✪ Why doesn't Gwyn tell Alison what he knows about Bertram? Do you think there may be some connection between Margaret and Bertram?

We see Gwyn's determination in the way he has made plans for what to do if he has to leave school. Notice how he has thought about each step. If he has to work behind the counter in the Co-op, he will continue his education at night school. In addition, he has saved up and bought a set of records which *teach you to speak properly*. He feels that learning to speak differently and going to night school will make up for leaving school . ✪ Do you sympathise with him? Gwyn says to Alison that it's easy for someone who doesn't speak in the same way as him to say that his way of talking doesn't matter. ✪ Do you think he should change his accent in order to 'get on' ? (Remember that the book was published in 1967. Attitudes to language may have changed since then).

Alison gives Gwyn the shell owl. ❂ Why does she want to give him something? Look at the writing on the box: A Kelticraft Souvenir. ❂ Why has the C in Celt been changed to a K? What impression do the manufacturers hope to give? Ironically, the object was 'Made in England'. Think about the ways in which the book makes us aware of the relationship between the Welsh and the English.

For you to do

? Before you go on, think about how the relationship between Alison and Gwyn is developing. What may be the effect of Gwyn confiding his feelings and plans to Alison? Jot down some of your ideas.

? Go back to your chart at the end of Chapter 12 showing what different people think of Huw. Add a column to show what the people in the valley think of him.

treat yourself to a short break – before more strange happenings in the next chapter!

Chapter 18

Something inside the stable room

◆ Roger and Clive hear noises inside the locked stable room.
◆ Clive tries to track down the lost key.
◆ Alison is disturbed by Huw and Gwyn and smells petrol fumes.
◆ One of her photos shows a shape between the fir trees – Gwyn.

We see Clive and Roger complimenting each other on their table tennis ability. ❂ What does this tell you about their relationship? Clive thinks Roger is finding it difficult to get along with Margaret and Alison. Clive talks about *these things* being difficult at first, but says they usually turn out all right in the end. It is important to Clive that the new family gets on well. Clive can't consider cutting short the holiday. ✪ Who would object if they tried to change their plans? Roger is reluctant to develop Alison's photographs straight away, but agrees when Clive asks him to. ✪ What does Alison say that makes Clive intervene? What do you think Roger feels about Margaret's influence?

Roger asks Clive if he can hear someone in the stable room. ✪ Why does he ask Clive and not Alison? Look at the way Clive talks to Huw when he asks him for the key. His tone is brusque and authoritative, and he is furious when he doesn't get what he wants. He calls Huw *dense*, and thinks that the domestic staff are conspiring to make a fool of him.

Clive asks Alison how her mother is enjoying the holiday. ✪ What does this suggest to you about the relationship between Clive and Margaret? He thinks that Alison has seemed out of sorts lately. ✪ Why do you think Clive is worried about Alison? Alison says he is kind; she has also called him sweet. ✪ Do you agree with this description of Clive? Clive jokingly calls Alison Mata Hari when she tells him how kind he is. Mata Hari was a spy who used her attractiveness to men to gain secrets.

Roger jumps in when Clive criticises Huw, and says they are all mad. Notice the way Clive softens his own criticism a bit, and says they can't be as bad as Roger makes out. Roger describes the way Gwyn has been sitting and glowering in the kitchen garden every afternoon, and says this proves he is mad. He changes the subject when Alison defends Gwyn. Roger calls him *that Gwyn character.* ✪ Why does he refer to Gwyn in this way? Why has Gwyn been sitting in the garden?

Alison answers evasively when Clive talks about the locked stable room, and doesn't say she agrees that the *'she'* who threw away the key must be Nancy. Alison also implicitly defends Huw against Clive's accusation of playing him up when she says that his English isn't very good. Alison looks in the water of the fish tank trying to see if her reflection is the same one she saw from the bedroom window. ✪ What answer would she like? Notice that the smell of petrol fumes occurs more frequently now. ✪ What does it suggest to you?

In Alison's photograph, the figure between the trees is Gwyn. ❸ What does this suggest about Gwyn?

Your turn

Now spend 10 minutes working on your Mind Map of strange happenings. You might include

- the reflection in the water
- the smell and sound of the motorbike
- the shape between the trees – a figure with something like a spear, a motorbike, Gwyn.

take a break, then prepare for a betrayal

Chapter 19

The betrayal

◆ Gwyn feels Alison is avoiding him.
◆ Nancy says that she and Gwyn will leave in two days' time.
◆ Roger and Alison argue.
◆ Alison tells him about Gwyn's records.

Gwyn watches Alison's movements closely, waiting for a chance for them to meet. ❸ How do you think he feels when she doesn't turn up in the kitchen garden? When he sees her laughing with Clive he wants to destroy the present she gave him. ❸ Why does he want to do this? Nancy is furious with Gwyn, thinking that he has told Clive about the key. Look at the way Gwyn sits on the stairs with his head in his hands.

Roger says that Gwyn crying on the stairs is embarrassing. By showing his feelings like this, Gwyn is going against Roger's code of masculine behaviour. ❸ What do you think of Roger's attitude?

Alison touches a nerve in Roger when she asks if he cried when his mother left. ❸ What does Roger's response tell us? Alison points out that Clive has done well out of marrying her mother. She implies that Margaret's family thought Clive wasn't a suitable husband for Margaret. Her phrase *rough diamond* suggests that Clive may have a *sweet* character but that he doesn't have the right kind of background. ✪ What do you think of Alison's comments? Is she trying to hurt Roger? Do you think Alison is a snob? Roger responds bitterly, pointing out that Alison's mother married Clive very quickly after her husband died, and that she married him for his money.

Roger's descriptions of Gwyn, Nancy and Huw are very contemptuous. He calls Gwyn and Nancy *weirdos* and calls Huw a *moron* and *Baconbonce*. Look at the way he jokes about the house being a headquarters for crime. ✪ Who else makes this kind of joke? What might Roger feel when Alison says he's not funny? Alison points out that Gwyn is cleverer than Roger and that Roger couldn't have worked out what was happening with the plates. Roger admits that Gwyn is intelligent, but says he's *not one of us.* ✪ What does he mean by this? Do Roger and Alison both have the same attitude to social class?

Roger doesn't question the fact that he is expected to work in Clive's business when he finishes school. Even if Roger wanted to be a photographer, he isn't sure he could go against Clive's wishes. Alison doesn't know if she could go against what Margaret wants for her.✪ Do you think Roger and Alison are weak in being so strongly influenced by their parents?

Alison is very disturbed by what Gwyn has told her about his future plans. Roger is harsh and unsympathetic, and in her attempt to make him understand Gwyn's situation Alison tells Roger about Gwyn's elocution records and the fact that he hasn't got anything to play them on. Alison wants Roger to feel as she does, concerned for Gwyn and ashamed that she should have so much and him so little. Roger refuses to sympathise. ✪ Why does Roger have this attitude? Why is the smell of petrol so strong at this point?

More for you

? Take a few minutes to go back to your comments on Clive and Margaret, and add any information you have gained from this chapter.

? Think about Roger's feelings towards Gwyn. Here are some words which you might use to describe them. Choose the ones you think are most appropriate then draw a large circle and divide it into segments with a word in each. Make the size of the segment match the strength or importance of the feeling.

compassionate   resentful   admiring   jealous   scornful

wary   frightened   liking   contemptuous   rivalry

before the tension between Gwyn, Roger and Alison reaches its climax, take a break!

Chapter 20

Gwyn feels betrayed

◆ Alison tells Gwyn that her mother is making threats to stop her talking to him.
◆ Gwyn has discovered that Bertram was killed on a motorbike on the mountain pass.
◆ Roger mocks Gwyn about the elocution lessons.

Alison tells Gwyn that she hasn't kept their agreement to meet every day in the kitchen garden because Margaret saw her up the mountain with Gwyn and has threatened to make her leave the choir and the tennis club if she continues to talk to him. ✪ Do you sympathise with Alison here? What do these particular threats add to your knowledge of Alison's way of life? Gwyn can hardly believe that Alison is giving in to such threats. He reminds Alison of their time on the mountain, and the present she gave him. He feels that their relationship must be more important than the choir and the tennis club.

Notice that at this point Alison says it's also that she can't bear to see Margaret hurt or upset. ✪ Why does she add this? Do you think it's true? What makes Gwyn calm down? Alison becomes very distressed when Gwyn tries to persuade her to meet him the next day, his last.

Look at what we discover about Bertram's death. ✪ How does

this affect your response to the frequent references to a
motorbike?

Roger mocks Gwyn by calling out phrases like *How now
brown cow* and *The rain in Spain falls mainly on the plain*,
which are traditionally used in elocution classes to train vowel
sounds. He lets Gwyn know that he knows about the records.
He also refers to the shop that Gwyn will have to work in, and
uses words like *prole* and *oik* to make fun of his working-class
background.

Gwyn is devastated. He can't believe that Alison told
Roger something he told her in confidence. He thinks
Alison couldn't wait to have a good laugh with Roger at his
expense. He backs away from the two of them, and Alison is
stricken by his expression and calls to Roger to make him stop
looking at her like that. Roger is triumphant. As Gwyn runs off
he can now reassure Alison and remind her that Gwyn is just a
yob. ❍ What are Gwyn's feelings? Do you sympathise with him?

Your turn

? Before you go on, think about the way Alison has
'betrayed' Gwyn to Roger. In the old legend, Lleu was
betrayed by Blodeuwedd. Are there any other ways in
which Gwyn is like Lleu? Jot them down.

? We can now see the link between the sound of the
motorbike, the shape of the motor bike between the
trees, the smell of petrol, and Bertram, who was
Nancy's lover. Add these ideas to your Mind Map of
strange happenings.

before we visit the Ravenstone, take a break

Chapter 21

The dogs

◆ Gwyn goes up the mountain to the Ravenstone.
◆ He notices the clover has not been flattened by his tread,
but springs back as he watches.
◆ He is driven back down the mountain by dogs.

We see Gwyn intent on getting up the mountain, out of the valley. He sees blades of clover spring back as if someone is treading on them. ✪ Where have we seen clover heads before in the book? What was strange about them? Notice that Gwyn isn't frightened, but just acknowledges the unseen presence. He feels lost amid the everlasting, desolate mountains and cries out for Alison.

The sheep moving across the slopes remind him of the joke he played on her. He stokes his anger and determination not to go back by thinking of his own trustworthiness not to reveal Alison's gullibility, and her humiliation of him.

The dogs come straight for Gwyn, called by the unseen men. They rush him down the mountain then run off into the meadow. Gwyn is left tired and hungry, wondering how 'they' could have known where he was going and what he intended.

STYLE AND LANGUAGE

In this chapter the immensity and mystery of the mountains are strongly presented. **Repetition** and **rhythm** are used to this effect in phrases like *nothing but mountains away and away and away, but mountains with mountains behind them ...* The use of words such as *barren* and *desolation* creates an atmosphere of harshness and loneliness, emphasised by Gwyn's feeling that *There was nowhere in the world to go.* A powerful sense of unseen presences is created in *crowding the hills with ghosts.*

Now do this

Add the incidents with the clover flowers and the dogs to your Mind Map of strange events.

the next chapter continues to focus on Gwyn and Huw — take a break before reading on

Chapter 22

'We were fetching him down this afternoon'

◆ Roger and Clive disagree about dealing with Gwyn taking food and clothing.

◆ Huw comes looking for Gwyn; we learn that Huw was involved in getting Gwyn back.

Look at the number of clichés Clive uses as he tells Alison and Roger not to upset Nancy. He tells them to *tread a bit softly*, that things are *a bit dicey*, that the kitchen is Nancy's *stamping ground*. He tells Roger not to make a fuss about the missing items. This time, Roger doesn't just agree to what Clive wants. He speaks scathingly of Margaret and says she will just have to be upset. Clive is angry when Roger persists and is even harsh to Alison when she says it doesn't matter. Clive also tells Huw that he can't expect payment for overtime. ✪ What do you think about Clive's behaviour here? Does it surprise you?

Huw says that *'we'* fetched Gwyn down from the mountain that afternoon. In some places farmers talk about 'fetching down' the sheep from the mountain. ✪ How, then, does the phrase fit the way in which Gwyn has been brought down? ✪ Do Clive, Alison or Roger show any interest in or concern for Gwyn's actions? Huw says he has to help his uncle finish a job. ✪ Who is the uncle? What kind of work does Huw mean?

Over to you

Take 10 minutes or so to think about Clive. Go back to the list of statements about him at the end of the Chapter 3 section. Use them as a basis and make notes or a Mind Map of your impression of Clive's character and the way he is presented in the book.

some questions are answered in the next chapter. You've earned a rest before going on!

Chapter 23

On the Black Hiding

- ◆ Gwyn climbs the Black Hiding.
- ◆ The black sow tries to attack him.
- ◆ He waits in an oak tree until daylight.
- ◆ Huw finds him.

Gwyn wants to get away without being seen. He waits until dusk before climbing onto the rocks,. We see how difficult the climb is when he runs at the shale and is stuck two hundred feet up, clinging on with his hands and feet, and has to build himself up to get to the ledge. Look at the way he talks himself into making the final effort. ❍ Do you think Gwyn is brave? He is surprised to hear Huw singing at the foot of his tree. ❍ Who does Huw remind you of here? If you're not sure look back at the section headed 'The Mabinogion' on p. 2.

Now do this

Think about Gwyn's feelings at this point for Alison, Roger and Nancy. Jot down your ideas.

take a short break before learning more about Huw in the next chapter

Chapter 24

The spear head

(To p. 134, *'Say it's from me.'*)

- ◆ Huw tells Gwyn that he is needed in the valley.
- ◆ Gwyn was destined to go to the Black Hiding – he'd gone in the wrong direction the day before.
- ◆ He finds Gronw's spear head in the hollow at the root of the tree.
- ◆ Other objects are in the hollow, all painted with the same pattern of eyes and nose.

◆ Huw tells Gwyn that Nancy was part of the previous 'three'.

◆ Gwyn puts the owl in the hollow and takes a slate for Alison.

At first Gwyn refuses to accept that it is his destiny to have gone to the Black Hiding and to go back to the house. He gives logical explanations for how he came to be in this particular tree and doesn't accept that Huw knew exactly where he would be. ✪ Is it typical of Gwyn to react like this? What do you think he is feeling? When does he change his attitude?

The pattern on all the solid objects in the tree hollow is the simple impression of the top part of a face, which may be of a bird or a human. ✪ What does the pattern remind you of?

Huw makes Gwyn see that certain people are destined to become part of the myth, and that every time it happens three people suffer. Gwyn, Roger and Alison are suffering because Alison made the flowers into owls, unleashing the suffering

Blodeuwedd endured when she was turned into an owl and forced to hunt and destroy. ❂ What does Gwyn feel when he hears that Nancy was involved in a similar triangle?

Gwyn's father

(From p. 134, *'Gwyn hid the last pieces'*, to end of chapter.)

◆ Gwyn finds pieces of brake blocks in the hollow.
◆ Huw says he was jealous and took out the brake blocks from Bertram's motor bike.
◆ Gwyn has inherited the burden of the myth because he is Huw's son.

The details of Bertram's death are finally revealed. Look at the weight that is placed on Gwyn when Huw tells him he is lord of the valley and that he must release Blodeuwedd from her loneliness and her pain. You have already thought about Gwyn's physical courage. ❂ Do you think he is mentally and emotionally strong? Gwyn thinks that Bertram must have been his father. ❂ What do you think Gwyn feels when Huw tells him that he is his father? What does he now think about Nancy?

You may remember that in the ancient legend Gwydion and Lleu's mother were half brother and sister. ❂ What does this add to the tragedy of the story?

STYLE AND LANGUAGE

Parts of this chapter have a poetic rhythm and intensity which contrasts with Gwyn's robust, colloquial language when he talks about *spooks, a nasty pair of chompers,* and jokes about being heir to a couple of brake blocks. Look at how the description of the spear head as *a leaf of sculpted light and stone* creates a feeling of strength and delicacy. The musical and poetic quality of Huw's language is apparent in his repetitions like *him with the painting, him with the plates,* and in the lyrical way he talks about Nancy as *the winds of April,* and Bertram as *the dark raven of my unreason.*

Over to you

? If you haven't already decided what name to put in the triangle with Nancy and Bertram, put one in now.

? What does this chapter add to your knowledge and understanding of Huw and of Nancy?

have a short break, and be ready for a nasty surprise!

Chapter 25

The owl and the motorbike

- ◆ Roger unscrews the padlock of the stable door.
- ◆ The room contains a motorbike, and a stufffed owl in a case, surrounded by Alison's missing owls.
- ◆ There is a flower pattern in the dust springing from the owl.
- ◆ Nancy enters with a poker, breaks the glass case, and lashes at the the paper owls.

Throughout this chapter the rain falls relentlessly. Roger agrees with Clive's policy that they don't carry quarrels over to the next day, but he seems edgy and angry. When he finds the motorbike he assumes that Alison found it first and has been sneaking off to ride it. ○ Whose is it? How do you think it got into the room? Why is the room kept locked?

Notice that the owl is called the Bryn Ghost. ✪ How do you think it came to be in the case, in the house?

For the first time Roger acknowledges the mystery of the house and valley, when he sees that the dust around the motorbike is disturbed only by the owl tracks. He says that something is up, and is alerted to a sense of danger. Nancy's sudden appearance is dramatic and threatening. The sight of her leaping and lashing out with the poker, surrounded by flying paper birds and covered with sawdust and feathers from the stuffed owl is haunting and macabre. The dramatic effect is increased by the use of sounds as all we can hear is her breathing, the whip of the poker, and her feet on wood and glass. ✪ Why is Nancy behaving in this way?

You may have thought of a possible connection, between Margaret and Nancy and Bertram. Gwyn thought that Bertram was his father. ✪ Could Margaret also have suspected this?

Alison's father is dead when the story begins. ✪ Could Bertram have been her real father? If Margaret knew that this might be the case, think about how this might affect her attitude to the friendship between Alison and Gwyn. (There is more about this in the 'Topics for discussion' section, p. 78.)

Test yourself

All the sets of relationships share certain characteristics. Write words from the following lists under the group of three people they most apply to.

Blodeuwedd, Lleu, Gronw		Nancy, Huw, Bertram		Alison, Gwyn Roger
love	hatred	jealousy	evil
possessiveness	power	deception	freedom
wickedness	anger	desire	betrayal
loss	pain	happiness	contentment
forgiveness	courage	death	destruction

treat yourself to a break before going on to see what happens to Nancy

Chapter 26

Nancy leaves again

- ◆ Nancy wants to leave straight away.
- ◆ Gwyn wants to stay but gives in when she hits him.
- ◆ They walk in a downpour to phone for a taxi to go to the station.
- ◆ Fallen trees block each road out of the village.
- ◆ Nancy leaves to walk over the pass and Gwyn stays.

Gwyn tries to stand up to Nancy, saying he wants to stay with his father and, unlike the way Huw behaved, face up to what is happening. The rain is a powerful force, so strong that it is visible in the sky, turning streams into waterfalls and creating danger of floods. It may be what causes the trees to fall and block the way to the station. ✪ What else might have caused this? Are Gwyn and Nancy supposed to leave the valley? Nancy is determined to go. The references to her *haunted face* and her *wild eyed* expression show us how desperate she is. She disappears to find her way over the pass in the driving rain, unable to stay. ✪ Why does Gwyn not go with her?

The villagers act as a kind of chorus, commenting on Nancy and her behaviour. They tell us that Nancy has always been headstrong and that she gets her own way. They encourage her to stay, and Gwyn to stay and look after her. Their attitude implies that Nancy belongs in the valley.

Think about

Alan Garner said he thought it was a mistake to include the villagers and the taxi driver. What do you think? Do these extra 'outside' characters lessen the impact? Write a paragraph giving your views.

Chapter 27

The power in Alison

(To p. 152, 'I've finished.')

◆ Alison runs after Gwyn and Nancy.
◆ Huw intercepts her and takes her to his room in the stables.
◆ He gives Alison the slate from Gwyn - she faints.
◆ Roger fetches Gwyn.
◆ Blodeuwedd's power is in Alison.
◆ Gwyn refuses to help.

Alison's first thought when she sees Gwyn and Nancy going is that *Mummy will be livid.* ✪ Why does she run after them? Huw is certain that they will be back. ✪ How does he know? Look at the description of the sack Huw is wearing. ✪ What does it make you think of? The sense that Huw is a part of the valley is enhanced by the way he seems to *grow out of the rain and stone,* and says he has *all the valley to keep things in.* Huw knows that *she's loose* now that the room has been unlocked. ✪ Do you think Huw knew that this would happen? Alison is very distressed when he gives her the present from Gwyn. ✪ What do you think she is feeling?

Roger is alarmed at the sight of Alison being carried over Huw's shoulder and her scratched face. ✪ What do you associate with the scratches? He ignores Huw's order to fetch Gwyn and tries to get a doctor for Alison. Mrs Richards in the shop knows that it is Gwyn who is needed. This adds to our sense that these events are anticipated and inevitable, and that they are moving towards a climax. Roger finds Gwyn at the very moment he is climbing over the gate from the road, having watched Nancy leave. ✪ Do you think it is just a lucky coincidence that the timing is so precise?

As Gwyn runs through the wood towards the house, the sound of the wind and the rain merges and echoes in the valley, becoming the noise of owls hunting. The feathers from the stuffed owl cling to Alison, although Huw keeps brushing them off her. The power invested in Blodeuwedd is now in Alison, and the forces of the old legend are being played out through her and Gwyn and Roger.

Think how Lleu and Gronw destroyed each other, how Huw destroyed Bertram and himself experienced his 'ending' through Nancy's betrayal. ✪ What does this suggest about Gwyn and Roger? We see Gwyn's bitterness in his refusal to help. He feels loyalty to Huw and the valley, but is angry with Alison and Roger.

'As easy as that'

(From p. 152, *Roger brushed the feathers away from Alison*, to end.)

◆ The feathers surround Alison, endlessly forming the owl pattern.
◆ More marks appear under her skin.
◆ Roger tells Gwyn Alison hadn't betrayed him.
◆ Gwyn uses knowledge of Roger's mother to hurt Roger.
◆ Roger suddenly understands that the owls should be flowers.
◆ His words calm Alison and the feathers turn into flowers.

The tension builds up as the feathers circle and cling to Alison, forming over and over again the familiar patterns of eyes and wings. The drama increases as the wind lashes the house and the rain comes through the skylight. The violence of the storm outside reflects the emotional turmoil inside. Alison is in great distress, crying and trembling as claw marks score her skin. We see that Huw knows what should be done, but can't do it himself. He urges Gwyn to get rid of his hate and give Alison the comfort she needs, but Gwyn can't. He hangs on to his bitterness as a kind of protection.

The final confrontation between Gwyn and Roger shows the depth of Gwyn's hurt. He rejects Roger's explanation that Alison wasn't laughing at him, and uses the knowledge he got from Alison to wound Roger in his most vulnerable area, his feelings about his mother. Roger accepts Gwyn's attack just as Gronw accepted the spear which killed him, and at last the pain and anger fade. Roger feels compassion for Gwyn and Huw. ✪ Does Roger's reaction surprise you? Alison becomes herself again as Roger tells her she's flowers, not owls, and says that all she had to do was make the pattern on the dinner service flowers. He is the one to show the understanding and tenderness necessary to release Blodeuwedd from the cruelty of owls and restore her to flowers. Gwyn remains cold and unforgiving. As Roger speaks the atmosphere is transformed into one of gentleness and beauty as the feathers become the fragrant petals of broom meadowsweet and oak, the flowers out of which Blodeuwedd was created.

The three of them have played their parts in the re-enactment of the age-old tragedy. ✪ Do you feel that the past has now been laid to rest for good, or only until another generation is caught up in its power?

Conclusion

Do you find this a satisfying ending? Roger suddenly emerges at the end of the book as decisive and courageous. You may remember him earlier admiring Gronw because he was the only one *with any real guts*. ✪ Do your feelings for Roger change? What do you feel at the end for him and for Gwyn? Jot down or Mind Map your response.

TOPICS FOR DISCUSSION AND BRAINSTORMING

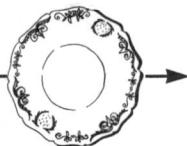

One of the best ways to revise is with one or more friends. Even if you're with someone who hardly knows the text you're studying, you'll find that having to explain things to your friend will help you to organise your own thoughts and memorise key points. If you're with someone who has studied the text, you'll find that the things you can't remember are different from the things your friend can't remember – so you'll help each other.

Discussion will also help you to develop interesting new ideas that perhaps neither of you would have had alone. Use a **brainstorming** approach to tackle any of the topics listed below. Allow yourself to share whatever ideas come into your head – however silly they seem. This will get you thinking creatively.

Whether alone or with a friend, use Mind Mapping (see p. iv) to help you brainstorm and organise your ideas. If with a friend, use a large sheet of paper and thick coloured pens.

Any of the topics below could feature in an exam paper, but even if you think you've found one in your actual exam, be sure to answer the precise question given.

TOPICS

1 What do you think of Clive and the way he is presented in the novel?

2 What do you find interesting about Gwyn's feelings and behaviour?

3 Do you find Alison a likeable character?

4 With which character in the novel do you feel most sympathy? Give reasons for your choice by referring to the text.

5 Choose two passages in *The Owl Service* where Garner has created strong mood and atmosphere. Write about each and discuss how the effect is created.

6 Roger says about Huw, 'The man's off his head.' Do you agree? Write about the part Huw plays in the book and give your views.

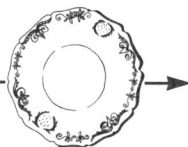

In all your study, in coursework, and in exams, be aware of the following:

- **Characterisation** – the characters and how we know about them (e.g. what they say and do, how the author describes them), their relationships, and how they develop.
- **Plot and structure** – what happens and how it is organised into parts or episodes.
- **Setting and atmosphere** – the changing scene and how it reflects the story (e.g. a rugged landscape and storm reflecting a character's emotional difficulties).
- **Style and language** – the author's choice of words, and literary devices such as imagery, and how these reflect the mood.
- **Viewpoint** – how the story is told (e.g. through an imaginary narrator, or in the third person but through the eyes of one character – 'She was furious – how dare he!').
- **Social and historical context** – influences on the author (see 'Background' in this guide).

Develop your ability to:

- Relate **detail** to **broader content, meaning and style**.
- Show understanding of the author's **intentions, technique and meaning** (brief and appropriate comparisons with other works by the same author will gain marks).
- Give **personal response and interpretation**, backed up by **examples** and short **quotations**.
- **Evaluate** the author's achievement (how far does the author succeed and why?)

THE EXAM ESSAY

You will probably have about an hour for one essay. It is worth spending about 10 minutes planning it. An excellent way to do this is in the three stages below.

1 **Mind Map** your ideas, without worrying about their order yet.
2 **Order** the relevant ideas (the ones that really relate to the question) by numbering them in the order in which you will write the essay.
3 **Gather** your evidence and short quotes.

You could remember this as the **MOG** technique. Then write the essay, allowing five minutres at the end for checking relevance, and spelling, grammar and punctuation. **Stick to the question**, and always **back up** your points with evidence in the form of examples and short quotations. Note: you can use '. . .' for unimportant words missed out in a quotation.

Model answer and plan

The next (and final) chapter consists of a model answer to an exam question on *The Owl Service*, together with the Mind Map and essay plan used to write it. Don't be put off if you think you couldn't write an essay as good as this one yet. This is a top 'A' grade essay – a standard at which to aim. You'll develop your skills if you work at them. Even if you're reading this the night before the exam, you can easily memorise the MOG technique in order to do your personal best.

The model answer and essay plan are good examples for you to follow, but don't try to learn them off by heart. It's better to pay close attention to the wording of the question you choose to answer in the exam, and allow Mind Mapping to help you think creatively.

Before reading the answer, you might like to do a plan of your own, then compare it with the example. The numbered points, with comments at the end, show why it's a good answer.

MODEL ANSWER

QUESTION

With which character in the novel do you feel least sympathy?

PLAN

1 Arrogant – rude to Nancy.

2 Snob.

3 Weak – influenced. Privileged and wants to remain so.

4 Her mother.

5 Bows to authority.

6 Patronises Clive.

7 Some sympathy.

8 Affection for Gwyn.

9 Betrays.

10 He can't forgive. Final judgement.

ESSAY

Although Alison has some painful experiences in the novel, I feel less sympathy towards her than to the other characters.[1] It is not her fault that she becomes obsessed with the pattern on the plates, but I dislike the way she speaks to Nancy when Nancy asks her for the plate. Here Alison appears rude and arrogant: 'Whose house is this, anyway?'[2] Her objections to Nancy's interference seem based on what she sees as Nancy's subservient position in the household: 'I don't have to take orders from my cook.'[3]

To some extent Alison can't be blamed for her snobbish attitude.[4] She is strongly influenced by her mother and has absorbed her ideas. We see this when she quotes Margaret about Roger's mother: 'Mummy said it was in all the papers,' and about Clive: 'Mummy's people were very surprised when she married him.'[5] She is always pleasant to Clive and tells him constantly how sweet and nice he is, but I feel her comments are slightly patronising, especially since she privately calls him 'a rough diamond'.[6] I think Alison is too weak to break away from her mother's influence, and she also enjoys her privileged way of life too much to jeopardise it. Margaret's threats to stop her membership of the tennis club and the choir if she continues her association with Gwyn are effective.

I do feel sympathy with Alison when she is compelled to make the owls and becomes more and more strongly associated with Blodeuwedd.[7] She is frightened by the power being released through her and tells Gwyn, 'Nothing's safe any more.' She is also a kind person. She defends Roger to Gwyn and says what a rough time he has had because of his mother. She is also very moved by Gwyn's situation, and is upset to think how easily things come to her and how hard Gwyn has to struggle.[8]

However, it is because of her relationship with Gwyn that I finally feel little sympathy for Alison.[9] She and Gwyn become very close, as can be seen in the afternoon on the mountain. They experience a range of emotions. They talk about their futures; Alison becomes scared when they discuss the reflection in the fish tank and asks Gwyn to help her; Gwyn teases her and makes her laugh; he explains to her about the power in the valley. Alison gives Gwyn the owl to say thank you for their time together. Because of their intimacy and trust in each other, it comes as a great shock when Alison reveals to Roger what Gwyn has told her. Even though she does not do this out of malice, but in an attempt to make Roger understand Gwyn's situation, I feel her action is a betrayal of Gwyn and of their friendship. As a result of this Gwyn withdraws from them and at the end of the novel is a deeply hurt, isolated figure, cold and unforgiving. I find it hard to forgive Alison for what she did, and so finally she is the character with whom I feel the least sympathy.[10]

WHAT'S SO GOOD ABOUT IT?

1 Focuses on question.
2 Knowledge of character and analysis supported by reference.
3 Interpretation based on text.
4 Develops argument.
5 Range of reference.
6 Personal response backed up by text.
7 Focus on question maintained.
8 Paragraph sustains argument.
9 Structure maintained and argument developed.
10 Gives clear reasons for choice. Personal response backed up by text. Shows interpretation and analysis.

GLOSSARY OF LITERARY TERMS

alliteration   repetition of a sound at the beginnings of words; e.g. burn, bubble.

context   the social and historical influences on the author.

image   a word picture used to make an idea come alive; e.g. a **metaphor**, **simile**, or **personification** (see separate entries).

imagery   the kind of word picture used to make an idea come alive.

irony   (dramatic) where at least one character is unaware of an important fact which the reader knows about, and which is somehow hinted at; (simple) ridiculing an opinion or belief by pretending to hold it, or pretending to be ignorant of the true facts.

metaphor   a description of a thing as if it were something essentially different but also in some way similar; e.g. a *foam of meadowsweet.*

myth   an ancient traditional story of gods and heroes, which has evolved over time, and which embodies popular ideas and beliefs.

personification   a description of something abstract as if it were a person.

simile   a comparison of two things which are different in most ways but similar in one important way; e.g. a river *sliding like oil.*

theme   an idea explored by an author; e.g. love and betrayal.

setting   the place and weather in which the action occurs, which usually affects the atmosphere; e.g. the valley, and the downpour in Chapter 26.

structure   how the plot is organised.

viewpoint   how the story is told; e.g. through action, or in discussion between minor characters.

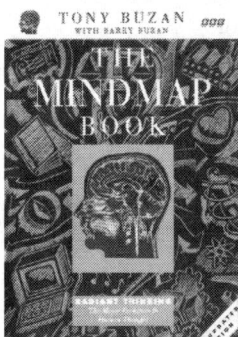